M.A.

M.H.

MARGOT STARBUCK

Foreword by TONY CAMPOLO

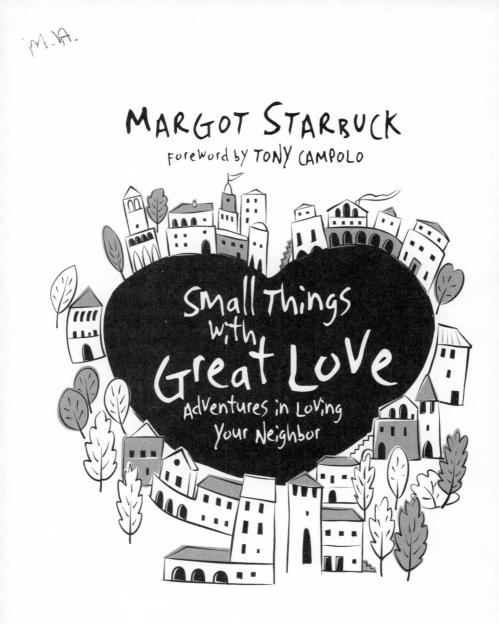

Small Things
with
Great Love

Adventures in Loving
Your Neighbor

IVP Books

An imprint of InterVarsity Press
Downers Grove, Illinois

InterVarsity Press
P.O. Box 1400, Downers Grove, IL 60515-1426
World Wide Web: www.ivpress.com
E-mail: email@ivpress.com

InterVarsity Press® is the book-publishing division of InterVarsity Christian Fellowship/USA®, a movement of students and faculty active on campus at hundreds of universities, colleges and schools of nursing in the United States of America, and a member movement of the International Fellowship of Evangelical Students. For information about local and regional activities, write Public Relations Dept., InterVarsity Christian Fellowship/USA, 6400 Schroeder Rd., P.O. Box 7895, Madison, WI 53707-7895, or visit the IVCF website at <www.intervarsity.org>.

Scripture quotations, unless otherwise noted, are from the New Revised Standard Version of the Bible, copyright 1989 by the Division of Christian Education of the National Council of the Churches of Christ in the USA. Used by permission. All rights reserved.

While all stories in this book are true, some names and identifying information in this book have been changed to protect the privacy of the individuals involved.

Design: Cindy Kiple
Images: © Sergio Bellotto/iStockphoto

ISBN 978-0-8308-3817-2

Printed in the United States of America ∞

Library of Congress Cataloging-in-Publication Data

Starbuck, Margot, 1969-
  Small things with great love: adventures in loving your neighbor /
Margot Starbuck.
      p. cm.
  Includes bibliographical references (p.)
  ISBN 978-0-8308-3817-2 (pbk.: alk. paper)
  1. Christian life. 2. Love—Religious aspects—Christianity. 3.
Interpersonal relations—Religious aspects—Christianity. I. Title.
  BV4639.S685 2011
  248.4—dc23

                                                                        2011032884

P	18	17	16	15	14	13	12	11	10	9	8	7	6	5		
Y	26	25	24	23	22	21	20	19	18	17	16	15	14	13		

For my Boompa,

who for ninety-seven years has engaged with the ones Jesus loves

without ever once having to write or talk about it.

CONTENTS

FOREWORD

I AM OLD ENOUGH TO REMEMBER when caring for poor and oppressed people—or at least feeling guilty about not caring—wasn't a very high priority for middle-class Christians.

Back in the days before overseas mission trips and inner-city summer programs became basic expectations for youth group kids, before Christian colleges began offering courses dealing with racism and sexism and cultural imperialism, before economic development and social justice entered the vocabularies of pastors and missions committee members everywhere, we church folks concentrated on more pressing questions: Could we serve real Communion wine instead of grape juice? Was Christian rock and roll music a dangerous compromise? Was it wrong to use any Bible translation other than the King James Version?

Oh, some of us were always out there, waving our arms and shouting about Jesus and justice and poverty and the kingdom of God, but we felt like sideshow performers, far from the center of the action. At some point, however, things began to change. Ron Sider's *Rich Christians in an Age of Hunger* jump-started the conversation among evangelicals; Dorothy Day and then Mother Teresa inspired the Catholics. Church people started listening to John Perkins and Jim Wallis and Bruce Ritter.

It didn't happen quickly or easily, but it happened: the rest of us figured out that the gospel of Jesus isn't just about getting people to heaven. The gospel of Jesus is also about letting the Holy Spirit use us to make this world the kingdom of God, which means it is also about you and me actually and practically loving our brothers and sisters in need.

The problem, of course, is that most of us don't have a clue about where and how to start. We know Jesus calls us to care for the poor and the oppressed—but we don't know where to find such people, let alone how to care for them. Or do we?

For many years I have done my best to motivate Christians to build the kingdom of God by reaching out to people in need. Some of those people have banded together to start inner-city youth groups, orphanages in Africa, literacy centers in Haiti, AIDS hospices and other wonderful ministry programs. From them I hear great testimonies of the glory of love. I hear other testimonies, however, from people who feel alone or afraid, or who simply want to do more.

If you want to experience the glory of love for yourself, then this is your lucky book. If you have been looking for a wise, understanding, thoughtful, encouraging, experienced and very funny people-lover to talk you through the process of getting into people-loving yourself, then Margot Starbuck is your lucky friend. Here is a real woman of God who doesn't pretend to have all the answers or to be especially holy or to be unbelievably sacrificial, but who has a unique and very helpful angle on getting better at the stuff that matters most. Margot is one of the up-and-coming leaders of a generation of Christians—the kind of people she and I call Red Letter Christians—who are taking seriously the red letters of the Bible and trying to live out what Jesus commanded his followers to do in his name. In this book, Margot deals with how to be a radical follower of Jesus while living what some might say are ordinary lives. Her insights make what is often ordinary living into something extraordinary, if the values of Jesus are implemented in the home and in the workplace.

I am old enough to remember when a book like this wouldn't have been possible, or very much in demand in any case, and when an incredible leader like Margot wouldn't have been possible either. Thank God those days are over.

Tony Campolo

PREFACE

Navigating This Adventure Book

THERE ARE THREE EASY WAYS to move through this adventure book!

For linear left-brainers:

1. Read straight through.

For creative-thinking right-brainers:

2. At the end of each chapter, read the instructions and choose which chapter to read next. It's pretty self-explanatory.

3. Once you've hopped through the book as *yourself*, read it again as someone else. Choose the next leg of your adventure as if you were your grandpa. Or your boss. Be your fifth-grade teacher. Or your postal carrier. You won't want to miss the relevant material in the chapters that aren't tailor-written for your demographic.

INTRODUCTION

My Reluctance About Following Super-Jesus

TOO OFTEN, I HAVE FAILED to engage with a world in need.

I've done it quite sincerely, especially when I've cloaked someone like Martin Luther King Jr. or Mother Teresa as a red-caped, neighbor-loving superhero. This convenient posturing inoculates me against actually doing anything. Rather, the unspoken assumption becomes that, since I'm just a regular gal, I *obviously* won't be doing anything superhuman like demonstrating for garbage workers or touching the pus-filled wounds of a dying stranger. This way I'm able to feel warm and fuzzy inside, admiring my heroes without the complication of actually joining them. Don't even get me started with Super-Jesus. Basically, if I make loving the poor a *big* thing, then I'm off the hook.

I think Mother Teresa must have known how I'd try to weasel around Jesus' clear invitation to engage with a world in need. So she said, "We cannot do great things, only small things with great love." Small things happen when I learn the name of my daughter's school bus driver. Small things happen when I listen to the dreams of a woman who lives in a group home on my block. Small things happen when I risk crossing a language barrier even though I look really stupid doing it. Small things, of course, put me back on the hook.

MY FRIEND HUGH

So if engaging with a world in need feels overwhelming to you, I get that.

Because managing laundry, a Visa bill, email and dinner are already unwieldy enough, entering into relationship with someone who is poor can feel more than a little daunting. This awareness is never more palpable than when I think of my friend Hugh, who shares life with folks who are homeless in nearby Raleigh, North Carolina. When I think of Hugh, I can start to feel guilty as I mentally scroll through all the ways I'm *not* engaged with the poor.[1] This list is quite extensive.

Recently Hugh had a chance to share with one local church that was filled with very well-meaning people. He challenged them to consider investing in relationships that cross boundaries of shelter and race and religion and income and class. One churchy guy there named Chuck was inspired by the vision. Like me, he'd bought into the big *idea* about Christians loving folks who live on the margins; at the same time, he wanted Hugh to hear what his life was like.

"I commute at least one hour, each way, to my job," explained Chuck. "I work at Research Triangle Park. I love what I do and I

---

[1] I use "the poor" here and elsewhere with some reservation. It's a designation that has, until now, been in common usage; it's also the language Jesus used. That said, I hope and believe we're moving *away* from language—"the poor," "the marginalized," "the oppressed"—that can subtly dehumanize people by identifying them by the challenges they face. Instead of "the homeless," try out "people who live outside." I know, I know; it sounds corny at first. Instead of "illegal immigrants," try "people who have immigrated without legal documentation." Naming beloved individuals as people *first* humanizes them in your own heart and in the hearts of others. The big idea of this book, of course—which is even better than finding just the right language to talk *about* people—is that you will begin to know these ones God loves *by name*. Baby steps.

work hard at it. The one day of the week I do have at home with my family, I don't want to go to the park and meet homeless people."

Often it's best to just lay it out there.

Hugh thought for a moment, and then asked Chuck, "Do you have an office?"

"Yes . . ." Chuck replied, not sure where this was heading.

Hugh continued, "Is there someone who cleans your office?"

"Yes," Chuck carefully answered again. "There's a woman who cleans my office two or three times a week."

"What's her name?" Hugh asked.

"I don't know her name," Chuck admitted.

Hugh pressed, "How long has she been cleaning your office?"

"Seven or eight years," Chuck estimated. By this point he was beginning to catch on.

Several weeks later, Hugh answered his ringing phone and heard a voice blurt out, "Her name is Regina!" Chuck had taken the time to meet the woman who cleaned his office, and he had learned that Regina was working two jobs to provide for her children.

"You know this has messed me up, right?" Chuck demanded of Hugh. By "messed up," he meant that being in relationship with Regina had sort of ruffled the comfortable, insulated life he'd been enjoying.

Smiling to himself, Hugh acknowledged, "I know."

You want to know just how messed up Chuck's life got? Chuck's family and Regina's family spent Christmas together last year.

It was a holy mess.

BUT WAIT, WAIT . . .

Before cuing the violin music, I want to say that I think Chuck made a pretty valid point about his regular responsibilities.

The formative reality for many of us is that, at the end of the day, we're too exhausted to get up off the couch after watching *Modern Family*, let alone garner the energy to go out and make new friends. Although we're not proud of it, the daily reality of our lives is that lawn-mowing and grocery-shopping and oil-changing and laundry-folding really *do* demand our energy and attention. Faced with our own needs and the needs of the world, we attend to that which seems most urgent. Then, with whatever energy is left, we feel bad about it.

For most of us, there just aren't enough hours in the day to have a cookout with our families *and* feed the poor. We don't have enough energy to do all our errands at Home Depot and Walmart and also care about adequate shelter and clothing for those in need. When we've got to choose between laying out two thousand bucks on car repairs or scraping together enough to buy a reliable used vehicle, we're not exactly pining for the kinds of new friends who'll inevitably ask us for rides. Though we certainly admire and applaud the modern saints like Hugh who engage in relationship with the poor *professionally*—in inner-city neighborhoods and on the foreign mission field—our daily lives are of a different order.

Our lives are already full.

They're not full of bad stuff, either. No square on my calendar reminds me to commit a homicide or torture cute Dalmatian puppies. In fact, one reminder prompts me to coordinate the nursery volunteers at my church. A few more squares on my calendar remind me to take walks with friends. Several have me scheduled to take care of other people's children after school. One means I get to eat a yummy dinner, cooked by my husband, with neighbors who are local grad students. I like that one a lot. Another has me meeting and praying with the church small group that meets in my home. A bunch of squares remind me to drive or fly places to talk about God, and even how much God loves the poor.

No one would say that my life is not full of good stuff.

THE $100,000 QUESTION

Here's the rub: a lot of us with rich, full lives do take seriously Jesus' command to love our neighbors the way we love ourselves. We're even willing to entertain the probability that his signature "good Samaritan" definition of *neighbor* calls us to befriend the unlikely and sometimes inconvenient type of person he describes in the story. And so the rich, full lives we lead, packed with important stuff—but without much margin left over to know those who live on the world's margins—sort of begs an important question.

Is God scowling in judgment because we're changing the batteries in our smoke detectors instead of going door to door collecting eyeglasses to send to Haiti? Is God looking down from heaven feeling sort of resentful that we're using the "look inside" function on Amazon.com instead of visiting prisoners? Isn't God angry that Americans keep getting fatter while so many on the globe are starving? You'd think so, right? A world in which a God who loves the poor would be a little bent out of shape that the rest of us are so darn self-involved is pretty imaginable.

And though it's certainly easy to conjure up that kind of a heavenly dichotomy, I simply don't think it's the case. Here's why: God's love for you and God's love for the larger world in need cannot be separated. God's longing to see you liberated for life that really is life can't be neatly pulled apart from God's longing to see the poor liberated for life that really is life. The two are inextricable. God's concern for the stuff of our lives, and God's concern for the lives of those who live on the margins, can never be neatly parsed. Wess Stafford, president of Compassion International, sees this pretty clearly. Wess will be the first one to tell you, "Compassion's work—releasing children from poverty in Jesus' name—is releasing me from wealth in Jesus' name."

That's God's big plan.

If your life is anything like mine, God longs to set you free from addictions to pleasure, appearances, busyness, consumption, envy, greed and self-absorption. I don't think it will come as a surprise that those sorts of miracles, until now, haven't been happening while we're at the mall or the movie theater or the nail parlor. Yet that's exactly where they're meant to happen.

For example, I can't say for certain that the good Samaritan, who helped the poor guy on the side of the road, *wasn't* on his way to coffee at the Jericho Mall to discuss a possible business merger. It's not like he produced a celebrity telethon or even launched a nonprofit to provide medical supports to mugging victims. He was just on his way somewhere—Target? Dentist appointment? Starbucks?—recognized someone in need and pulled over his donkey to check it out.

Can you see what great news it is that this serendipitous double liberation isn't something extra we do? We don't have to add lots more overwhelming activity to what we've already got going. Rather, the regular stuff of our lives—the commute to work and the potlucks and home improvement projects and errands and play dates—are the exact places in which we express and experience God's love for a world in need.

For instance, a conviction that Jesus' love crosses social and cultural boundaries informs which one of the parents in my daughter's kindergarten class I telephone to arrange an afterschool play date. It influences my husband's decision to direct his giving dollars toward a local ministry that's reaching teens who are marginalized by poverty, violence and lack of opportunity. God's heart for those on the world's margins affects the way my friend Suzanna interacts with the friendly, slow-talking young man who bags her groceries.

Who do you imagine when you think of those who live on the world's margins? Close your eyes for a moment and visualize these precious ones that Jesus called "the poor." Who do you see? What do they look like? If you are privileged—by race or status or income or gender—you may find that you think of non-white minorities. If this is true of you, *own* it.

I only mention this because, if you're anything at all like me, you'll want to deny or minimize noticing this as quickly as possible.

Can I help it if the folks I know who are poor just happen to be black and Latino? That's just the way it *is*.

When I look at the planet, many of those who do suffer poverty and oppression *are* people with lots of melanin.

But Jesus crossed barriers of race and gender and ethnicity and religion. I'm just acting like *Jesus*.

Right, right, right. I get all that stuff. And while it all may be *technically* true, it's still sticky business since even my impulse to "serve" is tainted with my own twisty racialized motives. Despite the fact that I'm quick to invoke Jesus' name, there can be a wily dynamic at work by which my "service" to "the poor" still allows me to feel superior to those I'm serving.

It's a mess, right?

In my own heart, this devilish bind can precipitate one of two things. It can paralyze me so that, stuck, I stay trapped in my privilege-ghetto, segregated from so many that God loves. But acknowledging the mess can also drive me to prayer when I recognize that the tainted kind of power I do have—by virtue of race and education and affluence—only interferes with, rather than lubricates, authentic kingdom relationships. Then, to get unstuck, I cry out, "God, be merciful to me, a sinner!" (Luke 18:13). This is pretty much how it goes.

Come, Lord Jesus.

Finally humbled, I realize that embracing the adventure of loving a world in need is—at its best—about giving Jesus, in us, access, through us, to the ones around us he already loves.

It's about doing small things with great love.

Ready to do this thing? Keep reading.

THE PLAN

Biggest Loser Wins

THE BIGGEST LOSER WINS.

That's the whole premise of the popular weight-loss reality show featuring women and men who are hundreds of pounds overweight. Whoever loses the most, wins. Every week, as someone is voted off of the weight-loss ranch, a compassionate host must confirm, "You are *not* the biggest loser." Dejected, the not-loser packs up his or her belongings and heads home.

If the scene feels weirdly familiar, it's because it's a story that's been told before. In Matthew 25, Jesus describes a divine host who gathers all the contestants and divides them up into two teams. Up until then, they'd all been living and dining and working out together in one big group. The host forms a red team on his right and a blue team on his left. And although the show's producer knows how the cut was made, the participants aren't yet privy to the behind-the-scenes priorities.

Then the host turns to the red team and says, "You win! You're the biggest losers! You lost your life, for *me*. You saw me hungry and shared your healthy snacks. When I was thirsty, you offered me your water bottle. When I was brand-new here, you welcomed me. When the airline lost my luggage, you shared your clothes. When I was sick, stuck in my room, you visited me. Even when I landed in jail, you visited."

The red team then looks at the host, feeling confused. "Um . . .

did all that stuff even *happen?* We don't really know you that well—probably because you're the celebrity and we're just regular people dressed in red T-shirts. We actually don't remember doing any of that stuff."

"What you didn't realize," the host explains patiently, "is that my kid brother, Marquez, who suffered a brain injury when we were kids, is on the food service crew. So whatever you did for those guys, you did for me."

Slowly, the red team catches on. Thinking back, they recognize that they sort of had done all that the host had mentioned. That very morning, in fact, when local cops had mistakenly picked up his brother, they'd gone to bail him out at the police station.

Then, the host turns to the blue team. "You're finished, gang. I was famished while you feasted. I was thirsty while you drank your pricey flavored vitamin waters. I was in need and you ignored me."

Because a lot of the folks wearing blue had been sucking up to the show's host all along, they were particularly confused.

"Um," they asked, "when did we see you have any of those needs and not help you?"

The host explained, "Whatever you didn't do for the folks who cleaned the rooms where you've been sleeping, the ones washing your dishes, the ones working in wardrobe—not to mention the undocumented ones living in trailers along the route where you jog who'd love to have any of those jobs—you didn't do for me. I'm sorry to tell you, blue team, you are *not* the biggest losers."

In the weird kingdom reversal, those who gave their lives away kept them, and those who clung to their own lives lost them. The blue team, disappointed, packed up their belongings and headed off dejectedly to eternal damnation. The red team, now sharing the stage with the gracious host, started jumping up and down, waving their new friends—the camera operators and paper pushers and the wait staff and the cleaning crew—onto the stage to share in the shower of confetti.

NOT A HUGE LOSS

Once you've grieved the disappointing ending for the blue team, you're left with the gospel-driven men and women on the red team who are daily choosing to lose their own lives for the sake of the ones Jesus loves. In this kingdom reversal, whether a relationship elevates one's own status or meets one's own needs becomes less important than the ways it confirms the inherent worth of another and satisfies his or her needs. Giving one's life away in relationship with those in need—according to Jesus—is the way to gain it. Whoever loses the most *wins*.

That said, we're not talking about huge losses here. We're talking about grabbing two sub sandwiches from the grocery store and sharing one with someone you just met who is really hungry. It might be offering some cold lemonade to the recent immigrant who's been mowing your lawn all morning. Inviting a stranger in might be as manageable as opening your dinner table once a quarter to foreign students attending a local university. Clothing the naked might just mean you quietly slip the athletic director at your kids' school—or *your* school!—some extra cash for the players who can't afford to pay for pricey uniforms. Visiting those in need could mean that you have coffee at the nursing home with an elderly woman from your church and then give her a ride to visit her son, who is doing time in prison for white-collar crime.

This is how *Kingdom Losers* is played.

If I were putting together an all-star team of kingdom players, it's these kingdom losers in red who jump immediately to mind. I'm thinking of Coach D, who pours her life into students who did not succeed in traditional schools. I'm thinking about Wesley, whose kids miss naptimes because a friendship has developed with a family who recently emigrated from Syria. I'm thinking of

Sarah, who gives her energy to women who are currently incarcerated. I'm thinking of all the folks who, like Jesus, see and know
and love those on the world's margins.

Go Losers!

TWO LOCAL LOSERS

My sons are losers. They are. Specifically, they are losers of stuff.
They don't lose Legos or remote-control vehicles or action figures;
somehow those stay permanently affixed to the floors of our home.
Put a sweatshirt on one of my boys and send him out the door to
be educated or play soccer, however, and that garment is as good
as gone.

I've tried all the things parents try. I wrote names and phone
numbers with fat black pens. I nagged my boys. I reminded others
to nag them. I threatened. Because none of these proved effective,
we eventually ended up layering long-sleeved T-shirts and any
sweater we could find. Now the sweaters are missing.

On a particularly bad week, my youngest son lost three sweatshirts. Three. One had been a hand-me-down, one had been a gift
and one my husband had foolishly purchased at an actual store.
Each time I fly, I scour the Sky Mall catalog for some sweatshirt-
locator device. I want there to be a discrete safety pin with a locator
chip, like they put in dogs, so that we can track down these sweatshirts. Inevitably, the locator costs more than the sweatshirt.

Clearly, I'm pretty driven to hold onto stuff. I'd rather keep my
stuff than lose it. I'd rather keep my life than lose it. Unless you're
an eight-year-old boy, being okay with losing stuff can feel pretty
counterintuitive. Jesus, though, has been pretty clear—both in
word and deed—that losing your life, for the sake of others, is the
way to go.

LEGITIMATE AND ILLEGITIMATE FEAR

A few weeks ago, after a late-night flight, I had to walk through a dark parking structure at the airport to get to my car. As scenes from every scary movie I've ever seen flashed through my mind, I clutched my keys in my right palm, ready to scrape the face off of anyone who tried to mess with me. As I approached my car, a man was waiting for me in the shadows, holding jumper cables and asking me for a jump. A surge of fear and adrenaline shot through my veins. Noticing the man's pilot hat and uniform, I quickly deduced that he was either a pilot or one very clever predator. After we spoke, however, I realized that he didn't mean to be a creepy man waiting in the shadows; it's just where his car had died while he was piloting other travelers across the country.

Fear, in a poorly lit parking garage, was a very appropriate and life-preserving response to the unknown in this situation. Too often, though, we have the same reaction to folks out in broad daylight whom Jesus would love to get close to, through us. These are the ones who elicit in us—by their need or by their difference— the same fearful fight-or-flight response.

In his Pulitzer Prize–winning *The Denial of Death*, Ernest Becker describes how human beings are moved in the most primal ways by fear—in particular, by our fear of death. If perchance you do not self-identify as someone who is afraid of death—either because you don't have a terminal disease or are not pushing your ninth decade or simply because you don't give death much thought on a daily basis—please keep reading.

Whether or not we recognize it, this impulse—to protect ourselves from the threat of death—influences everything from where we buy a home, to why we stay in jobs we hate, to who we invite over for coffee, to why we suddenly stop scheduling flights that land at midnight. Naturally wired to preserve our own lives, we are moved by an almost imperceptible fear of death. Toward this end, we often pick neighborhoods that are "safe," jobs that are "secure," friends who are "similar" to us and travel plans that are "sound." In choosing that which is familiar and promises to satisfy our needs, we fortify ourselves against dissonance, difference and, ultimately, death. Once we become alert to the impact of this fearful drive toward self-preservation, we begin to recognize it in all sorts of places.

That impulse to protect ourselves from those who make us anxious is palpable when we cross paths with a stranger in a dark parking garage. We notice it when we slow our cars to a stop too close to a weathered woman holding a cardboard sign asking for food or cash. We become aware of it as we pay attention to our gut reaction to the Middle Eastern man boarding a 747 next to us. When approaching a gang of urban teenagers on the sidewalk who we have decided look like trouble, we feel our heart rate increase. Too often, to protect ourselves from the anxiety evoked by strangers, we insulate ourselves from interacting with those we identify by their difference.

We do the same thing when we avoid folks whose needs—their explicit entanglement with the powers of death—evoke our anxiety. Though we have good intentions of visiting a neighbor in the hospital, time slips by before we ever do. Though we mean to care for a colleague who is grieving, we fill our schedules with other things. Though we long to support a friend going through a divorce, we remain at arm's length. And though we know that Jesus has called us to visit a classmate who is recovering from an emotional breakdown, weeks limp along and we never quite get around to it. Wired to preserve our own lives, we're moved—and unmoved—by fear.

HAVING WHAT IT TAKES

I only mention this primal human tendency because of Jesus. Rather than being driven by the natural anxieties that propel so many of us, he moved through the world and into relationships pretty fearlessly. Instead of being repelled by those marked by difference or by need, he was attracted to them and gave little thought to his own comfort, reputation or security. Again and again in the Gospels, we see Jesus moving toward those who— by their gender or disability or pain or sin or religious prefer- ence—seem most unlikely.

Today, as captain of the red-team losers, he invites those of us who want to play for his team to lose our lives instead of secure them. When we are no longer driven by self-preservation, Jesus moves in and through us to engage with others across natural bar- riers. What this means is that our lives—at work, at home, at school—start to look more like his. Instead of backing away from the kind of needy ones who can make the rest of us so uncomfort- able—the deaf, the blind, the sick, the lepers, the demon- possessed—we make a point, like Jesus did, of moving toward them. At church, we step toward the brother in personal crisis. In our neighborhoods, we embrace the single mom struggling to feed and clothe her children. In our communities, we respond with as- sistance to a report in the local paper about the ones nearby whose home burned down.

You might think that to live fearlessly like this you'd need a big old injection of courage. If you've ever seen *The Wizard of Oz*, you know that this would be a reasonable guess. To live fearlessly in relationship with others, however, doesn't depend on courage. Fa- thers who rush into burning buildings to save their children, wives in accidents who lift automobiles off of their husbands and friends who keep one another alive in an air pocket under an avalanche of snow—such people aren't moved by courage at all. They're moved by love.

So are those who try to pattern their lives after Jesus.

That said, I'm delighted to announce that all this movement to- ward beloved strangers doesn't depend on our love. If it depended on my love for someone I don't even know, the stranger and I would both be up fear creek without a paddle. Instead, courageous self- giving love depends on God's unshakable love for us and God's unwavering love for those in need. Just as the Father's love drove Jesus to be *for* you and me, his love is exactly what drives us from comfort to be *for* the ones God loves who are in need.

Jesus invites those of us who are weary from our hectic schedules and harried commutes and the burden of taking care of so much stuff into an entirely new way of living. Whether we run an office or wipe runny noses, we whose plates are already full—literally and figuratively—experience real relief in yoking ourselves to Jesus by moving toward the ones he loves. As we extend small acts of self-giving love in the course of our normal daily routines, God's kingdom comes on earth as it is in heaven.

I can hear how it kind of sounds too good to be true, and almost magical, and sort of like wishful thinking. A healthy dose of skepticism is in good order. The kingdom reality, though, is that the same gospel that is good news for me and for you is inextricable from the one that is good news for the poor. His name is Jesus, and he's inviting you into the upside-down, big-loser adventure of life that really is life.

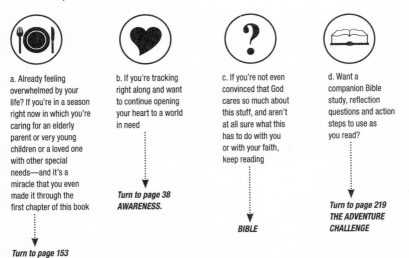

a. Already feeling overwhelmed by your life? If you're in a season right now in which you're caring for an elderly parent or very young children or a loved one with other special needs—and it's a miracle that you even made it through the first chapter of this book

Turn to page 153
CAREGIVER

b. If you're tracking right along and want to continue opening your heart to a world in need

Turn to page 38
AWARENESS.

c. If you're not even convinced that God cares so much about this stuff, and aren't at all sure what this has to do with you or with your faith, keep reading

BIBLE

d. Want a companion Bible study, reflection questions and action steps to use as you read?

Turn to page 219
THE ADVENTURE
CHALLENGE

••••••••••••••••••••••••••••••••••••• **2** •••••••••••••••••••••••••••••••••••••

BIBLE

Everyone Knows the Bible Is About *Spiritual* Things . . .

PERHAPS **YOU'RE THINKING,** *I'm just not sure why I have to be in relationship with people who are poor. They'd probably prefer to be friends among themselves, anyway. Is it even in the Bible?*

I hear you. It's just wack, right? I don't even have time to get to know all the fantastic people at my own church! So I can hardly be expected to go traipsing off in search of *new* friends. People who are poor probably wouldn't even like me, or my music, or my sense of humor, or my great shoes, or my grilled cheese sandwiches. I'll bet they'd have way more fun with friends who live in their own neighborhoods and go to their own churches than they would with dopey old me anyway.

THE CASE AGAINST THE POOR

Besides, the Bible isn't supposed to prescribe who to have coffee with or who you exercise with or who you invite to dinner. The Bible is about *spiritual* things. It's about Jesus coming to earth, dying on the cross and saving people's souls. Every good American Christian knows that. Oh sure, liberals will pull out a few verses to support their radical social agenda, but a lot of these passages shouldn't be taken at face value. This is why we have Bible scholars—to help us interpret the more murky texts. These passages need to be filtered—like yucky tap water—to make sure they're safe for consumption.

For instance, what about the one in which God instructs people, repeatedly, to care for the orphan and the widow? I'm willing to concede that this was necessary in ancient Near Eastern culture, since they didn't have Child Protective Services or Social Security back then. Which is probably why God included that important commandment. For them. These days, though, we don't have to get involved with any actual widows or orphans ourselves.

Or what about Mary's unbridled explosion when she announces that God "has filled the hungry with good things, and sent the rich away empty" (Luke 1:53)? That one has red flags all over it. Since women typically weren't very educated back then, she might have just been spouting off the cuff and probably didn't know for sure.

Sometimes lefties will quote Jesus, saying, "Blessed are you who are poor." What they don't realize is that Jesus was talking about *spiritual* poverty, not the regular old kind. Matthew's Gospel got Jesus right by saying, "Blessed are the poor *in spirit*" (Matthew 5:3). I'm not trying to be judgmental. It's very easy to imagine how maybe Luke stopped paying attention and just didn't jot it all down right. Throughout his entire Gospel.

As for Jesus spending *time* with the poor, that's just because they were everywhere back then, like a plague of locusts. He probably couldn't help it. If they'd had their own ghettos back then and hadn't been scattered in with the rest of the general population, Jesus might not have had to bump into them on roads and next to wells and temples. Today he'd probably just frequent the same coffee shops and malls and bars that *we* do and then wouldn't have to interact with the needy so much.

Those of us with a high view of Scripture realize that some of these texts simply cannot be entrusted to the average reader. I'm not saying that the typical churchgoer can't read *any* of Scripture. Not at all. In fact, I feel pretty comfortable letting allegorical and metaphoric texts stand on their own. Most folks can safely grasp that God is a rock or a king or a light. All of those broad, sweeping generalizations are pretty straightforward.

Oddly, it's those passages that have to do with the way Jesus talked about the poor and welcomed them and invited us to be with them that can be so easily misunderstood. Here's a convenient rule of thumb I've discovered for the times when I feel painted into a corner by Scripture: the more straightforward Jesus is, the more plainly he speaks, the more *wary* we need to be. Right?

For example, one of these stories that needs an awful lot of unpacking is the one Luke tells about Jesus encountering a rich young ruler. After asking Jesus what he must do to inherit eternal life, the guy walks away sad because Jesus asked him to sell his stuff and give the money to the poor.

I mean, what even *is* a rich young ruler? A twenty-eight-year-old senator? A child king? The ambiguity alone should probably disqualify the passage for serious inquiry from the get-go. The only thing I *am* clear about is that I'm not a rich young ruler.

I am not rich, because I have relatives and neighbors and church friends who make a *lot* more than I do. Seriously, if you're looking for rich, it's not me. I'm not young. I *used* to be pretty young, for several entire decades, but alas, I am no longer. Now I'm sort of . . . well, middle-ish. And I promise you, I rule over nothing. If I wielded any authority whatsoever, I'd be able to get my kids to pick their dirty socks up off the floor. I feel certain that Jesus' little tirade was meant for someone who actually has authority.

Don't get me wrong: I still believe this quaint vignette has got to be important for some reason. It's in the Bible, after all. I'm a big believer in the Bible. So I'll have a powerful spiritual encounter with the text, noticing how Jesus really turns the screws on *other* folks. This is just one of those passages that is so situated in a particular cultural context—like an Old Testament prohibition against wearing a cotton-polyester blend—that we shouldn't take it too literally.

Perhaps the irrelevance of this story to our lives will be more evident if we unpack it a bit.

THE POOR RICH GUY

Jesus is busy touching and blessing infants when a guy approaches him. At first this fellow sounds a little bit like a tricky brownnoser; he asks Jesus what he must do to inherit eternal life when everybody already knows that you're supposed to keep the commandments. So when Jesus rattles off half of the Big Ten, the guy responds smugly, "Done."

It's never quite so simple, though, with Jesus.

"There is still one thing lacking," Jesus continues.

If I were the guy—which, I believe I've made clear, I'm obviously not—I'd be hoping that the last little thing was something easy, like fetching Jesus a bottle of Evian or reciting some verse I'd learned as a kid at Vacation Bible School.

"Sell all that you own," Jesus explains, "and distribute the money to the poor, and you will have treasure in heaven; then come, follow me" (Luke 18:22).

That is so much worse than the bottle of water.

And this is the point in the story where I realize—from the guy's response—that he probably isn't a smart aleck at all. He isn't one of those stereotypical Bible bad guys who tries to trap Jesus or get him arrested. When Jesus says something that *those* religious guys don't like, they just stomp off angry to plot further evil to destroy him. Not our guy, though.

"But when he heard this," Luke explains, "he became sad" (Luke 18:23). The reason he was sad, says Luke, is because he was very rich.

Someone who thought Jesus was full of baloney wouldn't have been sad. In fact, he would have laughed. The *sad* is what makes me think this guy was genuine. It makes me think that he had really tasted life in Jesus and wanted to share the feast. In fact, I think that—without the whole "requisite sale" stipulation—this rich young ruler might have happily left his wealth in a secure IRA account and traipsed off after Jesus. Yet because Jesus' interest was in capturing the guy's *whole* heart, throwing off all that would encumber, the would-be disciple was sad.

I think that this man, like a lot of us, really wanted to follow Jesus. I think that's exactly why he was sad.

I also think that Jesus really wanted this guy to follow him. This wasn't busywork. Jesus really wanted the guy to be set free from his wealth to be with him and his other disciples. It wasn't a completely useless challenge that no one could actually achieve, like leapfrogging between large slippery obstacles on a Japanese game show might be. Jesus wanted the guy to be with him and his disciples as they fleshed out kingdom living together.

If we were taking things just at face value.

HENRI NOUWEN NEEDS MY HELP

Someone who probably needs my help in getting around the face-value interpretation of this Scripture is a writer named Henri Nouwen. The reason I think Nouwen needs my help is that, as a Catholic priest, he actually thinks he hears Jesus speaking to him in this passage, which is obviously only meant for rich young rulers.

In *The Road to Daybreak*, Nouwen explains, "When I look critically at my life, I give some of my money, some of my time, some of my energy, and some of my thoughts to God and others, but enough money, time, energy, and thoughts always remain to maintain my own security. Thus I never really give God a chance to show me his boundless love."

Because Nouwen doesn't seem to realize that Jesus is speaking to a very particular situation, he actually hears these words as a constant call to people like you and me, explaining, "Selling what you own, leaving your family and friends, and following Jesus is not a once-in-a-lifetime event. You must do it many times and in many different ways. And it certainly does not become any easier."

That unattentive guy is so silly sometimes. Because I'm pretty sure that this stuff-purge was a one-time deal for the young ruler. Then, after he'd proved himself by liquidating his assets and giving all he had to the poor, he'd join Jesus on his rigorous touring schedule.

For a long time I thought the young ruler had to do the overwhelmingly difficult thing—getting rid of all the stuff—in order to be eligible for the good thing—being in Jesus' inner circle. If I'd checked Jesus' itinerary though, and done the math, I might have noticed that "Part Two" only meant that the guy formerly known as Rich Young Ruler not only got to spend his *money* on the poor, but he'd also be spending his *time* among them. It's not like he was turning over the deed to his house in order to tour with Usher or Katy Perry. Nope. He was expected to do that weird thing for the privilege of being with Jesus, among the poor. The payoff was being in relationship with those on the world's margins.

All of a sudden giving up the stuff seems like the easier portion.

FOOD FOR THOUGHT

Since, when I'm not being facetious, I actually do believe that being in relationship with the poor is God's brainchild, here's what I suggest for those who are a little reluctant about this invitation to move, with Jesus, toward a world in need: read the Bible. (That, right there, was the not-facetious part. I know it's hard to tell.) Spend some time reading the Bible with a "Could it possibly be true?" attitude. With holy anticipation, ask, "Could it be true that God, who cares intimately about those who live with need, wants to be present to them through Jesus' life *in* and *through* me?" Approach the text with an open heart to this possibility: that the conditions of people's bodies and circumstances—whether they're hungry, sick, lonely, orphaned or widowed—is just as important to God as the condition of their souls.

Although it would be easy enough for me to proof-text some

verses and give you a big long list of them to look up, that's probably not so helpful. The best option would be for you to just read the whole big book from cover to cover, asking God, "Is this thing about building relationships with those on the world's margins where your heart is?"

Barring that unwieldy and admittedly time-consuming option, you might consider spending some time in:

1. The Psalms

   Notice the pervasive theme of God's heart for justice and God's concern for the weak.

2. A Gospel

   Try Luke. Notice Jesus' interactions with those who suffer. While our natural impulse may be to insulate ourselves from those in need, Jesus sort of gravitates toward these precious ones.

3. Deuteronomy

   No one ever recommends Deuteronomy as a good jumping-off point for enjoying the Bible. And for good reason. These rules and regulations God established for his people can be a little dry. Still, notice the ways that God provides for the weak ones— the stranger, orphan, widow—*through* his own people. (Really, that's his whole game plan.) Hint: Peek at chapters fifteen, sixteen and twenty-four.

4. The epistle of James

   Okay, okay, this one is a little proof-textish. Guilty. This letter, though, written around the middle of the first century, is just a great snapshot of the Christian life as Jesus' brother, James, understood it.

To discover very practical ways to begin to hold the world and its needs in your heart, keep reading **AWARENESS**. ⋯⋯⋯⋯⋯⋯⋯⋯⋯⋯⋯➤

AWARENESS

How I'm So Easily Overwhelmed by NPR

IF WE'RE GOING TO BUILD relationships with those in need, we sort of have to see them first. We need our eyes and ears opened to the presence of these beloved ones.

A while back, I found a few videos of my friend Chris Heuertz on YouTube and was enjoying watching them when I probably should have been doing something else.

It always feels less like wasting time when it's someone I know.

In one, Chris tells the story of John Wesley having returned home from the market with frames for a bunch of pictures for his walls. Wesley had just finished arranging everything in an aesthetically pleasing fashion when he heard a knock at the door. A woman stood in the freezing cold, holding a baby and begging for money. Reaching into his pocket, Wesley found only a few spare coins left after his shopping spree. He gave her what he had and sent her on her way.

Then, falling to the floor, Wesley was overcome with grief as he realized that the plunder of the poor described by the prophet Isaiah was in his house, hanging on his walls (Isaiah 3:14). He'd mistaken the resources with which he'd been entrusted for personal provision when they were really supposed to be for others, possibly the hungry little family that had just stepped off the porch.

And bummer for me that I was, at that very moment, hiding

away a gorgeous pricey painting I had commissioned a gifted artist friend to create for my husband's Christmas present. I was, of course, planning to hang it on the wall on Christmas morning, just like John Wesley.

Clearly, I hadn't planned on being spiritually convicted by watching YouTube that day. Had I seen it coming, I could just as easily have wasted time on Facebook.

EYES WIDE OPEN

The Holy Spirit's big business is to open our eyes and ears to the ones God loves who are in need. Although I know this, I typically do not want to be involved at all with the particulars of agony or injustice.

As a sensitive soul, I am simply much more comfortable not knowing some things. In particular, I am ashamed to admit at cocktail parties that I have not yet been able to stomach watching *Schindler's List, Hotel Rwanda* or *Precious*. I'm sort of a lightweight when it comes to other people's pain.

Another one of these distressing predicaments is a common injury that some women endure while giving birth, called fistula. Though no one's forcing me to watch it unfold on a wide screen for one hundred and nineteen minutes, I don't want to entertain the mental image for even two. Caused when bladder or rectal tissue is damaged during obstructed labor, fistula creates incontinence in women. Around the globe, many women without access to medical care suffer from this humiliating and devastating condition. I don't mean the occasional little drip while bouncing on the neighbor's trampoline; I mean that women have absolutely no control to hold in either urine or feces.

I didn't want to hear about obstetric fistula when my friend Martha, a physician working in global public health, described it on one of our morning walks. She ignored the fact that I was plugging my fingers in my ears and shouting, "La la la la la! I can't *hear* you!" Last month I did not want to read about it in a feature article in *Christianity Today*. Thankfully no diagrams or intimate illustrations were involved. I don't want to write about it now, when I could be wasting time on YouTube *and* Facebook. I'd much prefer to operate under a "don't learn," "don't think," "don't care" policy when it comes to fistula.

Am I heartless? Cruel? Although my children will, on occasion, beg to differ, I am typically neither. I do, though, have this whole queasiness situation going. Watching the discomfort of others makes me feel too . . . uncomfortable. Seriously, I can barely manage to watch the social awkwardness that unfolds on reruns of *The Office*. So avoiding both gyno-injuries and the documented cruelties of humanity is really all about managing my comfort level.

I don't want to feel . . . well, *bad*. So I keep myself from feeling bad as much as I'm able.

My sister, a medical student applying for an OB/GYN residency, visited this week, and I accidentally asked what her future might hold. Although she'll probably begin stateside, she explained, she'd also be open to the possibility of a public health assignment overseas working with indigenous women.

She began to explain, "Fistula is . . ."

"I know!" I barked. "I *know*!"

HEALTHY SPIRITUAL ARTERIES

Though clearly my temptation is to look away, I've learned how these things work. Hearts willing to see and hear, ones that respond to God's voice, stay pliable and usable; those that turn away become hardened. Although I'm not yet renting any of the traumatic DVDs, I did gather up all my resolve and slogged the entire way through *Christianity Today*'s fistula exposé.

Long before scientists had identified the menacing threat of hardened arteries, the God of Israel had spoken through prophets to warn against it. The softening and hardening of human hearts was a popular theme with these Old Testament prophets. According to divine cardiology, heart-hardening could be avoided by exercising justice and mercy as God's designated agents among the hungry, the orphaned, the fatherless, the strangers and the poor. Admittedly, that whole sequence involves actually recognizing injustice and human need in the first place.

The prescription reads: "This is what the LORD Almighty said: 'Administer true justice; show mercy and compassion to one another. Do not oppress the widow or the fatherless, the foreigner or the poor. Do not plot evil against each other'" (Zechariah 7:9-10 NIV). As is often still the case, that clever cure was easier said than done.

Like a disappointed nurse who has caught her cardiac patient scarfing onion rings and cheesy fries in the broom closet, Zechariah continues, "But they refused to pay attention; stubbornly they turned their backs and covered their ears. They made their hearts as hard as flint and would not listen to the law or to the words that the LORD Almighty had sent by his Spirit through the earlier prophets" (Zechariah 7:11-12 NIV). Hear that? Israel didn't, until it was too late. They refused to see and they refused to hear. The effect of Israel's failure resulted in a ruptured relationship not only with those in need but with the Lord.

Healthy, soft hearts see the need in the world that God sees. They see and respond. Hardened, crusty hearts just turn back to their own important, greasy, cheesy business.

Engaging a world in need begins as we allow ourselves, as we challenge ourselves, to see and to hear something new. Don't worry; this is much more manageable than it may sound at first. Sometimes recognizing the need is as simple as doing nothing.

SEEING, HEARING, KNOWING

For instance, on any given day I gun the gas pedal to make it through another yellow light in a frenzy to complete a list of local errands. After National Public Radio's fascinating feature on a day in the life of a circus clown, I continue to listen to the top stories of the day only because I think I should. Truthfully, the earnest words of the radio journalist blur in my ears as I'm assaulted by another news report heralding the planet's most recent tragedy. (I mentioned I'm a sensitive soul, right?) I can't even track whether it is hundreds or thousands who now suffer in the wake of the globe's most recent natural disaster. The remote geography and abstract statistics fail to inspire. If there were a convenient number to which I could text some token financial assistance, I might possibly remember to do it later. But there's no number. There's no order. There's not yet a plan for relief. As the news floods in, there is only chaos, pain and despair.

Short on both energy and imagination today, I will not be that lady whose neighborhood bake sale raises thirty thousand dollars for disaster relief. What I really want to do is shut off the radio.

I don't.

Today, bearing the weight of the world's agony will be enough.

Seeing, hearing and knowing is where discipleship begins.

As we purpose to truly see, hear, know and respond to others, we are imitating the divine pattern of engagement with those in need. In fact, this is the rhythm of God's own care for the Israelites who were enslaved in Egypt: "The Israelites groaned under their slavery, and cried out. Out of the slavery their cry for help rose up to God. God heard their groaning, and God remembered his covenant with Abraham, Isaac, and Jacob. God looked upon the Israelites, and God took notice of them" (Exodus 2:23-25).

God heard. God saw. God knew.

Admittedly, it gets a little nutty after this. This is when God appears to Moses in a burning bush: "Then the LORD said, 'I have observed the misery of my people who are in Egypt; I have heard their cry on account of their taskmasters. Indeed, I know their sufferings, and I have come down to deliver them from the Egyptians" (Exodus 3:7-8).

God saw. God heard. God knew. And I believe there was a mention that God was about to clean house. God's own relationship to a world in need is one in which God sees the conditions of those who suffer. God hears our cries. God knows the particularities of our circumstances, and God cares.

It's the holy pattern of engagement into which we, too, are invited.

FROM WHERE WE STAND

Since humans do come up so short on the omniscience front, the type of seeing and hearing and noticing to which we're called won't always fall right into our laps. Oh, sure, sometimes we'll accidentally see a moving bit on YouTube or in a magazine, but we probably shouldn't rely too much upon being accidentally inspired.

Bruce Main is the president of Urban Promise ministry, headquartered in Camden, New Jersey. Main describes an *active* awareness by citing the old Haitian proverb, "We see from where we stand." Main explains that when we change the places we stand, "our perceptions of the world will be changed and challenged." This has certainly been true for the hundreds of volunteers, like this one, that Urban Promise has welcomed to the city over the last several decades. It's been true of those who have visited Haiti since its devastating earthquake in January 2009. It's true of many who have traveled to places of desperate need, domestically and abroad. With a fresh perspective, the world begins to look different.

Where have you stood? Where do you stand?

If you grew up comfortably, went to college and got a job that pays the bills, you most likely see the world from atop well-heeled shoes. For many of us, the home, work and church ghetto where we spend most of our time does not naturally bring us face to face with those in need. The ones who share our homes, workplaces and church buildings are often not so socioeconomically different from us.

Thankfully, those of us who have lived comfy lives aren't disqualified from engaging with a world in need; we've just got to get a little more intentional about it. We can keep up to speed by reading news magazines. We can learn about global issues pretty easily by clicking the "About Us" tab on trusted ministry websites. We can keep our eyes open, locally, for folks in need.

This year I was given the opportunity to travel to El Salvador with Compassion International. The big idea was to witness the work of Compassion firsthand so I could share what I'd seen with others. This is really my kind of mission trip. I am *so* much better at paying attention to what I'm seeing and then sharing about it with others than I am at constructing anything resembling a dwelling. So it seemed like the right fit.

Standing on the ground in El Salvador, I could see and hear and taste and touch what was happening in the lives of children and teens. Not only was I afforded a glimpse into the sticky web of poverty, I also witnessed the impact of hope on those once tangled in it. Being with precious sisters and brothers, who were serving through their local churches as the hands and feet and voice of Jesus in the lives of children, was a true gift.

Although I could have read all that great stuff in a magazine, when I stood on the unpaved road in front of a local church, I saw the radiant delight of a mother beaming proudly at her son, who was on his way to college. I saw hope where there used to be no hope. I saw a future where there was once no future.

LOCAL OPPORTUNITY

I hope you did not just feel jealous of me because you may not have the opportunity any time soon to stand in an impoverished neighborhood in an exotic overseas location. While it's possible that

God may call you to view the world from El Salvadoran flip-flops, or Haitian ones, or Indian ones, it is an absolute *certainty* that God longs for you to experience a fresh perspective of the world from where you already are.

Maybe just pivot a little.

As you're willing to open your eyes and ears to the world's need, you open yourself up to relationship with the ones God loves.

a. To discover the unlikely folks we're meant to be in relationship with

b. To be safe, and to find out just who we are **not** talking about engaging in kingdom relationships

turn to page 50
STRANGER

keep reading
OUR OWN

4

OUR OWN

Final Flight Instructions

I'VE ALWAYS BEEN THAT PERSON on the airplane who dutifully gives the flight attendant some eye contact as she buckles a very short seat belt in the air or stretches an elastic band over her head without messing up her hair. Although I've been flying forever and know all the instructions, I want to encourage her by making my head and face look like I care. Even though it's now done on a video screen, I still look up out of habit.

"Please secure your own mask before helping others . . ."

On the tiny screen in front of me, as pixelated oxygen masks drop from the ceiling, a very calm mother applies and adjusts her own lifeline and then places a mask on the smiling child next to her. It's as if they're both about to go trick or treating.

Since they're not about to extort neighbors for candy, though, I have to remind myself at the onset of every single flight why on earth I should administer lifesaving oxygen to myself before offering it to my child. Why again? Invariably, I have to do the math to remember that I'm supposed to don my mask so that I'm able to help the child sitting next to me. The logic there is that if I were to get her masked up and then pass out, I'd be no good to her.

This least maternal of all acts is counterintuitive because, as a parent, the very *first* thing I'm going to do in the event of an emergency is help my child. If there's a train accident and he's pinned beneath thousands of pounds of steel, I'll throw an entire string of cars off him like I'm the Incredible Hulk. If there's an earthquake and dangerous debris is raining out of the air, I'll throw my body over hers. If there's famine and we have just a little bit of food, I'll feed it to him. I'm no hero; this is just what parents do.

So although year after year I have no trouble at all remembering that the nearest aircraft exit is possibly located behind me, I actually do need the reminder to help myself before helping my child. I need to be reminded because it's entirely counterintuitive.

IT'S ALL ABOUT ME

I'm not at all saying it's counterintuitive to look out for my own needs. That comes fairly naturally. I do that every single day of my life. When I'm hungry, I eat. When I'm thirsty, I drink. When I'm cold and I'm not feeling too lazy, I get a jacket. If I'm lonely, I call someone. If I'm sick, I drive to the drugstore and spare no expense on whatever potion or lotion will make me feel better. Believe me, I am all about me.

The *only* time my first instinct is to aid another before myself is when that Other is one of my own. When there are just three slivers of chocolate cake in the fridge and I know that my three hungry children are about to burst in the door after school, it's no sacrifice to forgo the cake. When my elderly grandparents are in need of a visit from someone who absolutely adores them, it feels mostly manageable to drive the twenty-four-hour roundtrip in a minivan with three active children strapped into car seats. When we're at the beach and my husband is super-thirsty, it's no big deal to hand him my water bottle, even if I know I'll be thirsty a while longer.

Please don't nominate me for any humanitarian awards, though, because sacrificing for my own isn't really so noble. Essentially, these ones who are known and loved by me are sort of an extension of myself. Since I'm pretty sure that this tribal instinct to protect and please ourselves and our own has gone a long way toward ensuring the survival of the species, I'm not knocking it.

I just don't think it's the end of the story.

That our own are those who share our DNA is just the beginning of the story.

That our own are the precious ones who have been adopted into our family forever is a given.

That our own are the fraternity brothers and sorority sisters who share the same weird rituals we do is just a starting point.

That our own are the friends at church who have become a new kind of family for us is foundational.

It ain't so hard at all to sacrifice for these, our own. The real kicker is that when we are entirely identified with the triune God, the ones who are *God's* own become *our* own.

The orphan, wherever he is found, becomes our own in exactly the same way that he is God's own.

The widow, the one who's been left alone, becomes our own just the way that she is God's own.

The hungry neighbor, across town and across the globe, becomes our own in the same way that he or she is God's own.

The sick, the ones who suffer, become our own in the same way that they are God's own.

The prisoner, the one who has been forgotten, becomes our own in exactly the same manner that he is God's own.

Now that's *something*.

OWN-NESS

My mom and I were thumbing through magazines at a new doctor's office when I was a teen. As I filled out the medical history questions, including family history, on the requisite new-patient clipboard, my mom looked up from her magazine to remind me, "Don't forget, I had ovarian cancer."

"Yeah . . ." I hedged carefully, "but I'm adopted . . ." I said it really gently, as if she were receiving the information for the first time.

That our DNA didn't correspond had entirely escaped her because, in no uncertain terms, I was her *own*.

Perhaps because I am adopted, one of my favorite moments in the movie *The Blind Side* was when the Tuohy family gathered around the dining room table to officially invite their house guest, Michael Oher, to become part of their family.

In lieu of either the joy or surprise one might expect, Michael instead looked confused, explaining, "I thought I already *was*." Because he'd been treated as their own, he naturally assumed he already *was* a member of their family.

This most Christian belonging to one another never diminishes one's identity. I suspect Michael Oher experienced this. Knowing himself to belong to his biological family in an intimate way, he also belonged to the Tuohy family.

As Jesus moved through villages and cities, he engaged with others—namely, *different* others—as if they were his own. If I had a magic looking glass, I would love to have seen the reactions of his friends and enemies as he moved in this very countercultural way.

I imagine the look of his disciples when they came back from the grocery store to find him chatting with a woman at a well who was, well, a woman. And a Samaritan. She was the wrong gender, wrong race and wrong religion. And yet Jesus treated her as if she were his own—which, of course, she was.

I imagine the crabby, judgmental looks on the faces of the religious authorities who caught Jesus partying with sinners. Did he not realize that his reputation, his own cleanliness, would be sullied by prostitutes and thieves? And yet Jesus treated them as if they were his own—which, of course, they were.

I imagine the look on the mugs of earnest religious women and men when Jesus both touched and was touched by the sick, the disabled, the leprous, the bleeding and the dirty. Apparently ignorant of disapproving eyes, Jesus treated the weak as if they were his own—which, of course, they were.

Like my mother, like Michael Oher, Jesus gave no apparent indication that a woman or man or child living on the world's so-called margins was anyone other than his own.

As we claim them, today, as our own, he recognizes us as his own.

To discover more about embracing the stranger as your own

keep reading
STRANGER ···➤

STRANGER

Why Jesus Crossed the Road and Why We Do

FOR MONTHS, AS I DROVE back and forth between my house and my church, I noticed an elderly woman collecting tin cans from curbside recycling bins. She wore simple slacks and an overcoat. Walking along the side of the road, she stooped at each blue recycling bucket to fish out cans and drop them into her own white garbage bag. Was she a sculptor of tin? Did she collect those little metal tabs? Did her new cardio workout require intermittent squats? I had no idea.

One day while taking a walk, finally liberated from my minivan, I was able to chat with this woman. I learned that Miss Sarah was unable to make ends meet while living on a fixed income. She was gathering aluminum cans to be recycled for change in order to supplement what she received each month. It was a scenario I had not imagined.

Although I saw her, physically, on a regular basis, I had no idea what life was like for my neighbor until I stood next to her and heard her story.

For too long, my neighbor was a stranger.

FACEBOOK FOLLOWERS AND CYBERSTALKERS

Though I'm not proud of it, more often than not, this is my story. I *want* to follow Jesus toward the beloved stranger but I'm slow to do it. An unfortunate vocabulary situation around the word *follow* only reinforces my naturally self-referenced bent.

When we follow people on Facebook or Twitter, we end up catching some of the random thoughts and links they toss into cyberspace. When we follow their blogs, diligently or intermittently, we might learn even more about what makes them tick. When we follow them online, we get to know them a bit better.

And because most of us know what it means to follow someone online, it's understandable how we might accidentally roll that definition over to our spiritual lives. As followers of Jesus, we catch some of the random thoughts and links to the Hebrew Scriptures that he tosses out. We learn what makes him tick. We can peek to find out where he grew up. If we're cyberstalkers, we'll even scroll through his photos and watch his videos.

What we don't do when we follow someone online, of course, is actually *follow* follow them. We don't physically follow them throughout their day. We don't hide behind a trash can in the alley behind their garage and wait for them to go someplace in their car. We don't track them as they duck in and out of grocery stores, laundromats and gas stations. We don't tail them on Saturday nights when they go out on dates. That would be weird.

People, it *is* weird.

Specifically, following Jesus—and encountering the same people he does—is going to look extra weird, because following him everywhere he goes inevitably leads us into relationship with strangers. For instance, some of the people today who follow Jesus into the homes of notorious sinners end up spending less time holding hymnals at church activities and more time holding cold beverages at parties. Some of these followers, like me, now spend less time in climate-controlled minivans and more time walking on actual sidewalks. They spend less time with people who look like them, think like them, talk like them and earn like them in order to spend more time with people who are just . . . different.

HOW MUCH TIME DOES JESUS SPEND AT TARGET?

But since these days we really can't see Jesus or hear him or smell him in the same way his first disciples did, literally following him can feel a little subjective. I mean, what are we even talking about? For instance, who's to say that you might not follow *your* Jesus across the border to the slums of Mexico while I sense *mine* leading me to the Target across town?

Although I can't say for certain that you won't find Jesus in Target, if you're following any deity who's leading you to retail outlets without leading you toward people, you might want to do some sort of an ID check. Jesus is all about people. He was even pretty clear that following him might lead someone *away* from their blood kin, and it almost always lands them among beloved strangers. When we follow him, that's where we end up too.

"But Margot," you may protest, "Jesus was with Bible strangers. Aren't those particular people, with whom Jesus consorted, lepers from two millennia ago? And aren't they overseas?"

That would be handy, wouldn't it? Then, if we didn't know any lepers, we'd sort of be off the hook. Or if the people Jesus loved were just out of chronological reach, then, conveniently, we'd be freed up a little bit for other stuff. Or if today they were geographically segregated to India, or Ethiopia or Haiti, then we'd have a legitimate excuse to avoid the strangers Jesus loves. Clearly, if you're scheduled to coach Little League this Saturday, then you simply cannot be crossing any roads or oceans or language barriers to follow Jesus toward the ancient people with whom he just naturally rubbed elbows.

If we equate Jesus' ancient neighbors—lepers and prostitutes and tax collectors and other unlikelies—with the neighbor we wave at in the next driveway as we're hopping into our fuel-efficient sedans, we've also misunderstood Jesus. A respectable first-century Jewish man would no more naturally rub elbows with any of those unsavory folks than you would in your cul-de-sac.

Jesus was, however, taking his cues from and following the lead of Another.

Jesus had studied the speech and gestures and expressions of his Father. He had watched him move toward the hungry, the captive, the naked, the homeless. He had paid attention when his Father reached out toward the poor, the prisoner and the brokenhearted. Because the heart of his Father clearly dwelled among these, Jesus moved toward them. His eyes rested upon them. His feet crossed roads to be with them. His hands touched and healed and fed them. Jesus' body literally tracked, followed and embraced the ones who dwelled in the center of his Father's heart. In this, his Father's own became *his* own. As we physically follow Jesus with our bodies, the stranger becomes our own as well.

CROSS THE ROAD TO THE BELOVED OTHER

If you think that the poor and weak and brokenhearted aren't residing in your daily orbit of influence, I'd challenge you to take another look. Although you might not have any clinically diagnosed lepers, I promise you that there are others—sick, lonely, poor, shunned—who are closer than you think. In *Friendship at the Margins*, Chris Heuertz and Christine Pohl invite us to open our eyes to the beloved strangers in our midst. They exhort, "Every community has people who are invisible or overlooked, and each of us can move toward wholeness through the friendships we offer and receive."

Yesterday I was driving downtown and I saw a woman I call "Zacchaeus" wearing a visor and bright yellow shirt duck into a drugstore. I do not believe that Zacchaeus is her given name, but it's what I call her. "Z" (for short) is the town's meter maid. By my reckoning, anyone who does nothing all day besides troll around looking for cars to ticket has got to be just as despised by her community as the first-century tax collector. At least by me anyway. I scowl at her even when I'm driving right past her and my car isn't anywhere near a parking space. My disdain came to a head a few years back because, while my church friends and I would be enjoying a powerful lesson at our women's Bible study, she'd be creeping around outside ticketing the cars of those who'd exceeded the two-hour street parking limit because they'd arrived early to set out freshly baked treats. If that's not persecution, I don't know what is.

Still, when I'm in my right Christian mind, I am certain that Jesus would beeline toward this modern yellow-shirted villain. And not simply because he didn't drive a car. This is his *girl*, and she was meant to be ours. Who else, in your own local orbit—by virtue of their occupation or personality or smell or bad habit—is Zacchaeusie? Who sort of repels more people than they attract?

This week you might encounter someone who lives with HIV/ AIDS. Or another one of these low-visibility strangers might be the man who walks the short distance from his nursing home to Whole Foods for a daily cup of coffee. Another might be a neighbor who lives with dementia. Or there may be a faithful employee who cleans your church every week to whom Jesus is calling you. Perhaps it's a child in the neighborhood whose parents are divorcing. Maybe it's the new Latino neighbor whose loud polka music is the hot topic on the neighborhood listserv. These who neither command nor demand our attention are the kinds of modern-day strangers where we meet, and are met by, Jesus.

Social homogeneity was never a value Jesus embraced. Instead, he purposefully crossed the natural human barriers of class, race, religion, gender, geography and age. As we begin to study his motions, and follow him with our bodies, we'll become barrier-crossers as well. My friend Bruce Main has identified this very movement in his book *Why Jesus Crossed the Road*. For Bruce, following Jesus across the roads that separate us from these beloved others transcends dutiful imitation and, in fact, ushers the road-crosser into authentic spiritual maturity. Maturity, for Main, means that we no longer separate the interior conviction that God is *for* the poor from a physical expression of that conviction with our time and bodies and resources. In this respect, followers of Jesus simply can't *not* be road-crossers.

Is crossing the road toward a beloved Other risky? Yes. Inconvenient? Terribly. Uncomfortable? Absolutely. If you leave your car parked on the other side for more than two hours, it can even get costly. And yet crossing the road to meet the stranger is the way we walk when we study and track and trail—when we *follow*—the person of Jesus. And while the risks of road-crossing are evident, the benefits might not be.

COST BENEFIT ANALYSIS

The perks of sidling up to the rich and famous are immediately apparent. We expect to get something from them. We hope for a little of their status to rub off on us, and we drop their names in enough conversations to convince others that it has.

The gifts of being among the poor and forgotten, however, can't be as easily anticipated. This isn't to say that they're not abundant, because they are. It's just to say that we can't control them the way we might like.

Heuertz and Pohl celebrate the way both parties are blessed when roads are crossed. Chris mentions opportunities he had to sit with Mother Teresa, explaining, "In meetings with her, she would frequently say, 'We need the poor more than the poor need us.'" Did you catch that? The big opportunity isn't for the weak ones, the vulnerable ones or the frail ones dying to be with a well-meaning American showing off a soothing waterfall app on her iPhone. The ones who receive, who are filled up in deep, unspeakable ways, are the ones who don't seem to be *physically* dying at all. Somehow, as we follow the person of Jesus, moving toward the ones with whom he spent time, we find life. This holy mystery is exactly what I'm talking about when I say that the gospel that's good news for the poor is good news for us too.

Please, don't take my word for it. Don't take Bruce's word for it, or Chris's. Just *try* to prove Mother Teresa a liar. Read the Gospels and discover for yourself how Jesus crossed all kinds of barriers to encounter the beloved stranger, the Other. If we really did follow this guy with our bodies, we'd be embracing, connecting, tear-drying, touching and throwing back a beer with people who'd make folks at our churches very uncomfortable.

Those aren't metaphors. We'd really be doing those things.

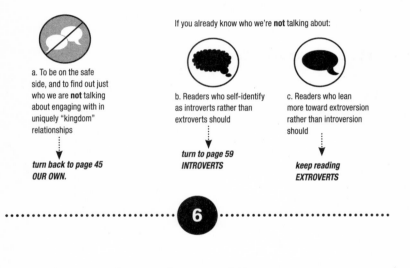

a. To be on the safe side, and to find out just who we are **not** talking about: engaging with in uniquely "kingdom" relationships

turn back to page 45
OUR OWN.

If you already know who we're **not** talking about:

b. Readers who self-identify as introverts rather than extroverts should

turn to page 59
INTROVERTS

c. Readers who lean more toward extroversion rather than introversion should

keep reading
EXTROVERTS

6

EXTROVERTS

Promise Not to Brag

Psst! Extroverts, promise me you will not brag about this around the introverts, but you bring something very particularly wonderful to the kingdom table God is setting. In fact, your gift is indispensable.

MY HUSBAND, AN EXTROVERT, belongs to the strain of extroverts who are naturally more cautious than adventurous. I do not believe there's a Myers-Briggs personality type featuring this *cautious* sub-designation. So while he's energized by being around others, he's not what you'd call a big risk-taker. In fact he's as socially, medically, politically and fiscally responsible and conscientious as he can be.

A few years back, when we visited my folks in Venice, California, Peter attended a church conference—or, rather, a not-churchy conference—called The Ooze. I think part of the big not-churchy idea was to get out beyond the church's walls and engage with folks who'd only be caught dead in a church.

One afternoon the conference participants headed out to the boardwalk to be with teens who lived at the beach: on the sand, in alleys and under tarps. Peter and a few others struck up a conversation with some guys who lived on the street. Everyone seemed to enjoy getting to know one another.

While they were hanging out, one of these guys headed off to the corner market to bring back a cold forty-ounce beer. Taking a deep drink, he passed it to the friend on his right. This guy, in turn, took a drink and kept passing it. When the shared can reached Peter, he had to decide whether or not to partake.

Did I mention this? This is the same guy who only received the bread, and not the communal cup, while receiving Communion at a church service in Haiti.

But suddenly struck with a pretty keen sense of what Jesus would do, he tipped his head back, took a drink and passed the can to the next guy.

This weird encounter symbolizes, for me, the uncomfortable adventure into which Jesus calls those who will pattern their lives after his. I carry it as a little kingdom snapshot, in my mind's eye, as I think about the kind of extrovert my husband was made to be. Sure, this guy who feeds off the energy of others can entertain a crowd at a cocktail party, but this road-crossing encounter with God's beloved ones is where he came, and where we come, face to face with Jesus. It's what he was made for.

ENERGY-FEEDERS

Though I understand it may be difficult for some of you extroverts to grasp, the casual beer circle—among strangers or intimate friends—is a nightmare for some of us introverts. It's not the germ factor either. Nope, we introverts are entirely depleted six minutes into church coffee hour, wouldn't be caught dead at a youth group overnight lock-in and would rather wear a sweater knit out of barbed wire than go to a drop-in holiday party. Extroverts, please hear that the fact that you're energized when you're engaged face to face with others is a real gift.

Sure, you *could* use the gift to schmooze with important people at exclusive events in order to claw your way up whatever ladder you're climbing. There's something even better, though, for you and for the world. Your mission, should you choose to accept it, is to use your powers to build kingdom relationships.

For instance, you model kingdom road-crossing when you invite the most unlikely ones, from church or work or the 'hood, to come and enjoy your dinner parties and barbecues and holiday celebrations.

You bridge barriers between cultures when you're willing to take a risk and employ your very weak command of the Spanish language to get to know the aide who cares for your ailing grandfather.

You build bridges of friendship when you grab two icy cold chocolate milks at the quick mart and then sit down and share one of them with the woman or man who asks for money at the traffic light near your office.

You break down walls when you spend time at a local high school, at football games and musicals and choir concerts, getting to know the kids who would otherwise be overlooked.

You actualize the vision of a kingdom in which all the typical stuff that separates people—clothing labels and car makers and street addresses and diplomas and paycheck stubs—is made irrelevant when human bonds are formed between actual breathing people. Across lines of religion, race, sexual orientation, tax brackets, gender, political preferences and all the other stuff that too often separates us, you're following in the footsteps of Jesus by making most of it completely subordinate to the more important thing of loving your unlikely neighbor.

Extroverts, you build the kingdom as you move toward the ones God loves.

I'm not even going to belabor this, because the bazillion ways that you can positively affect a world in need are so stinkin' obvious. I simply remind you to go do your friendly thing among the unlikely folks God loves.

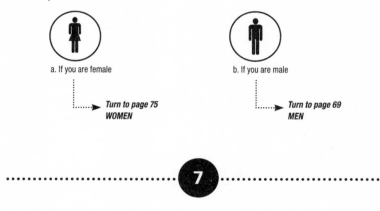

a. If you are female

............▶ *Turn to page 75*
WOMEN

b. If you are male

............▶ *Turn to page 69*
MEN

●●●●●●●●●●●●●●● **7** ●●●●●●●●●●●●●●●

INTROVERTS

If There's One Thing I Hate, It's a Party

Psst! Introverts, promise me you will not brag about this around the extroverts, but you bring something very particularly wonderful to the kingdom table God is setting. In fact, your gift is indispensable.

IF THERE'S ONE THING I HATE, it's a party. Seriously. I would rather be holed up in a dark room with my laptop than go to a party any day of the year. Any of my loved ones will confirm this.

It's not the confetti or Mylar balloons or salty snacks that keep me away. It's the *people*. They could be the most fabulous people on the planet, and usually are, and I'd still prefer to be in the quiet, secluded location.

Some folks are shocked by this news. "How can that be, Margot? As a professional speaker, you talk to lots and lots of people all the time, right?"

"Well," I explain, "when I'm talking into a microphone, how many other people are talking at the same time?"

"Hmmm . . ." they muse. "I guess it depends how boring you are."

"Let's say I'm *fascinating*."

"Well," they're forced to concede, "then there's probably no one else talking."

"Bingo! Want to see me dissolve into tears? Have two people raise their hands and start asking questions at the same time, hire a loud helicopter to fly by, arrange for someone's cell phone to start ringing a show tune and have a small child whine, 'Mah-ommm-mmmm.' I promise you I will curl up in a ball and cry."

"Wow. I can't wait to try that cool party trick."

YOUR NAME ON IT?

I'm sure there are a host of other reasons for my antisocial situation, not the least of which is the fact that my brain has serious trouble processing more than one sound at a time.

Here's the rub: if following Jesus leads us to love people—which the Gospels seem to reveal—then consistently choosing my laptop becomes problematic. If the two greatest commandments are to love God and love others, then refusing party invitations in order to sit at home alone, basking in screen-glow, might possibly miss the mark.

So I argue with God, "But it's how I *am*! Can I even help it if this is how I am?!?" This is how my whining sounds. "It's your fault, anyway," I reason, "because you made me this way."

Despite some thorough Bible-scouring, I've not yet found the passage that releases natural introverts from loving God and loving people. So the question then becomes, "How do I, Margot, who is overstimulated by too many sights and sounds, love God and love people? What does that look like?"

For starters, out of love for my husband, I sometimes go to parties. And I only gripe about what a big sacrifice I'm making for 87 percent of the ride there, until he gently requests that I take a break from all the crabbing. Then I stop.

Next, I do *not* volunteer as a fun middle-school youth group leader at church. I do *not* offer to put six seven-year-olds in my van and be the cool field-trip mom who drives three hours to the mountains. I am *not* the edgy missionary who hangs out at heavy metal bars to practice friendship evangelism. Truly, I could go on all day about all that I am not.

What it took me a few decades to learn is that by bravely owning all the things that I am decidedly *not*, I'm finally freed up to be the person God created me to be. I learned this from a brilliant down-to-earth woman at my church who starts out her many, many requests for folks to pitch in to help others with, "I've got something here and I want to see if it has your name on it." It isn't just the clever sentence that captures my imagination—which I have, indeed, memorized to use for my own personal advantage. Rather, it is Callie's clear conviction that

1. If this is God's work, then God will put somebody's name on it. God will gently tap someone who is gifted and called to do it. I'm very clear that someone—possibly you—might

very well be gifted to do this, and still not called to do this.

2. If it's *not* got your name on it, then don't bother hogging it up—out of some sort of misguided obligation—because it's meant for someone else. And it's better for everyone involved if you'd just kindly step out of the way.

Of course Callie doesn't say all the rude stuff, but that's the gist of it. It's contagious too. Now I get all sorts of phone calls and emails from others Callie has touched that extend to me this same grace-filled opportunity to care for needs within and outside of our body. When the need involves customizing a Monopoly game for sweet friends moving out of town, I freely say yes. When the need involves herding twenty squirrelly children for a week of Vacation Bible School, I say no. I hope you see the wonderful freedom in this.

I am completely clear now that, in lieu of doing some of that horribly exhausting and life-draining extrovert stuff, my job is to find *other* ways to use my time, resources, gifts and influence for the sake of the world God loves.

EXTROVERTED CHURCH

In his book *Introverts in the Church*, Adam McHugh argues that both the mission and the community of the evangelical church have traditionally been geared toward the extrovert. Think about zany pied-piper youth group leaders and folks who love sharing the gospel zealously at parades and football games. McHugh, himself a self-professed introvert, came close to bowing out of ordained ministry before he even began. He explains, "A subtle but insidious message can permeate these communities, a message that says God is most pleased with extroversion."

That stinks for us, right?

Those of us who are natural introverts can be drained by the world of people, things, activities and events while we're enlivened among the world of thoughts, feelings, imagination and ideas. Our growing edge, then, as those who follow after Jesus, is to find ways to love God and people, especially ones who are marginalized, that are appropriately suited to our temperaments. When I asked Adam what engaging with a world in need might look like for introverts, he offered three possible jumping-off points.

First, he points to the witness of Mother Teresa, and suggests caring for the person right in front of you. He explains, "That one-on-one-focused relationship is key for introverts."

He's right, I thought. *I can do that.*

He also suggests that introverts can participate in God's ministry to the world through intercessory prayer. Though Christians can sometimes behave as if prayer is sort of like buying travelers insurance before a mission trip, McHugh is convinced that prayer for God's world *is* the mission. "Prayer isn't just the *prologue*," he observes.

He's right, I thought. *I can do that.*

Finally, he points to the quiet ministry of servanthood. In contrast to some more flashy forms of ministry, McHugh invites introverts to smallness, acknowledging, "Great good can be done through small things and small steps."

Right again, I mused. Mother Teresa couldn't have said it better herself.

INTROVERTED ROAD-CROSSERS

At Urban Promise ministry in Camden, New Jersey, it's obvious how extroverts are loving a world in need. They're running camps and afterschool programs. They're building relationships with children and teens. They're taking high school students on trips to visit colleges. While it's admittedly fantastic stuff, this worthwhile stuff is altogether life-sucking and death-dealing for some of us introverts.

Because Bruce Main wrote a book called *Why Jesus Crossed the*

Road, I had to ask him what on earth road-crossing means for folks who aren't natural extroverts. When I did, Bruce pointed to the witness of some Urban Promise volunteers who are working with youth to build beautiful wooden sailboats. These aren't toy boats; they're boats for real people that actually float. With people in them.

Bruce offered, "I think of our volunteer boat-builders. In a social situation, with inner-city kids, these guys would be incredibly uncomfortable. But give them wood to cut, diagrams to read, epoxy to apply and they are comfortable, even with a kid hanging on their arm. So, I'd say that an activity of some sort might be helpful for the introverted type."

Perhaps you're not a skilled carpenter. Take some crayons and markers and paper to a domestic violence shelter and just get crafty. If you dance, take some music and teach the kids a routine. Heck, take your Wii, hook it up and play Just Dance. Doing an activity together is a great way to forge quiet, workable relationships.

Compassion International has a program for volunteers who are willing to write letters to sponsored children who aren't receiving regular correspondence from their own sponsors. As children share about their lives with these pen pals, in return, real relationships develop. Through this personal communication, children learn that they are not forgotten and that their lives matter. Introverts bless forgotten others as they take an interest in their lives.

Bruce, who recruits the introverted Urban Promise boat-builders, adds, "I think a big part of being effective road-crossers is the ability to listen. Introverted folks are often better listeners and actually tend to connect with the marginalized in ways that other folks can't." I do think he's on to something with this. Part of the reason I dread parties is because I fear I have to have just the right sparkling, witty words on the tip of my tongue. Which is way too much pressure. The gift introverts can give, especially to the people who are dodged and neglected and overlooked, is to *listen*. This is true at parties and churches and schools and, via pen and ink, in remote overseas locations.

My sweet friend Peggy does this beautifully. For years she has given herself to relationship with "old ladies." (Her words, not mine.) In fact, I am unclear whether or not the effervescent Peggy is aware that, in all the decades she's been giving herself in this way, she has sort of *become* an old lady. Today she pours herself into others by spending time with them and sending them notes in the mail. These women, who are so easily overlooked by a culture that's all about youth, beauty, pleasure and convenience, are reminded, by Peggy's gentle presence, that they are worthy of love and attention.

That said, it's *not* a one-way street. Peggy genuinely delights in these women just as they enjoy her visits. She explains, "They help me to figure out how I can best navigate the journey to being older and older. The truth is, I get more from most of them than I have ever given. My old lady friends are, to me, graduate school, and I thank them for that." This is the unexpected surprise of being among the powerless: as authentic relationships develop, preconceived ideas about who's the giver and who's the receiver begin to vanish.

Do you have a neighbor who visits a relative who is institutionalized? Tag along. Has someone you know ended up in an extended care facility? Lend an ear. Does someone in your church care for an ailing parent or grandparent? Take the time to sit and listen. Sure, it'll take some energy. Bruce Main explains, "Road-crossing is uncomfortable, but that's the point."

Point taken.

JOSLYN THE UNLIKELY HOUSE FLIPPER

The unique possibilities for introverts using their gifts to build kingdom relationships are endless. Trust me, I started to do the math and they are, literally, without end.

My husband loves—I mean really loves—houses. When we moved into our neighborhood, he even wanted to buy two of them so that he could fix one up and rent it out. Two. Because ours is a neighborhood in flux, he might even have been able to score a bargain—if we'd had an extra ninety thousand dollars lying around.

Personally, I'm glad we didn't, so we didn't thrust our neighborhood into even more, well, flux. My hope, and the dream of our local credit union, is that someone who has been renting in this neighborhood for twenty or thirty or forty years might be empowered to buy one of these available houses. That would be great, right? That's the dream.

My fear, though, is that folks just like my husband and me will recognize the ripe opportunity and gobble them all up as investments. That's just the way it works with folks of means who, if we don't have it in our personal piggy banks, can often find a way to garner the resources to make the purchase.

My precious friend Joslyn and her med-school husband recently completed a redeemed version of this very thing.

Joslyn, who is energized by lots of stuff other than crowds and parties, was the first person who alerted me to this situation of the church's ministry being extroverted. Sure enough, after she said it, I looked around and saw that she was exactly right. Then I read Adam McHugh's book and realized that these two were on to something *big*. Joslyn's dream, she'd shared with me, was to find a unique way to serve by weaving her particular combo of introverted gifts together to minister to a world in need.

That kind of dreaming and visioning was sort of the starter gift. The outcome—because she's like that Bible woman who is called blessed because she weaves cloth out of lint and wisely buys and sells stuff—was that Joslyn purchased an affordable home. Getting the house in decent working order, with her plentiful handywoman skills, was the third round of gift-using. Then she worked with a local agency that helps to transition families from

homelessness into homefulness to identify folks who could benefit from a gentle, loving transition into the responsibilities of renting a home.

Though it seems like I'm about to endorse Joslyn as a candidate for
some office, her fabulousness is not the point here. Nor, even, is the
success or failure of her venture, which turned out to be a much
bumpier adventure than she'd originally imagined. Rather, what is
truly noteworthy is simply that she recognized the way that God had
made her, prayerfully discerned how God might use that unique subset of gifts and then just stepped out into it, learning as she went.

Notice, discern, step. This is the holy rhythm into which disciples are invited to tread forward.

LOTS OF OPTIONS

Here are a few more ways introverts are affecting a world in need:

1. Blogging

Tap, tap, type, type. Humans at home, cuddled in couches and
squishy chairs, are typing away on their various blogs. Thousands and thousands of readers are catching the vision behind
various ministry efforts because these writer-types are using
their particular gifts in the comfort of their own living rooms. If
your gift is communicating, use it. Engage others with the ministry God is about in the world.

2. Letter Writing

When the lonely open their mailboxes, a personal letter reminds
them that they are not forgotten. A letter communicates to a
widowed aunt, a struggling nephew, a homesick soldier, a de-
pressed prisoner and a beloved grandparent that they matter
and that someone cares for them.

3. Apps

No, not iPhone apps. If you've benefited from any kind of post-
secondary formal education, you've filled out your fair share of

applications. The fact that you've navigated that nutty maze—from SATs, to college applications, to the FAFSA financial aid form, to scholarship applications—means that you have something to share. A student who represents the first generation in his family to go beyond high school could be blessed by you. This will be especially true if you've done it in the last five or ten years and did not individually chisel each personal essay onto rocks mined from your cave.

4. Paperwork

For some, the post-grad version of college apps is adoption paperwork. Many families with the desire to bring a waiting child into their home would be so blessed to have someone who has been through it guide them through the process. For me, that paperwork labor was like the pain of giving birth: once I held my child, I completely forgot about it. Literally, if I had to do it again I'd have absolutely no idea where to begin. If you retain more information than I do, please help someone else on the journey.

5. Foster Care and Adoption

Right now there are thousands of children in the United States who are in need of loving homes. There is a great need for families, couples and single folks to welcome children who are in foster care. Whether you're able to provide emergency care, respite weekends, long-term care or even adoption for children who have been legally released for adoption, you put flesh on God's love for the orphan when you love these precious ones.

Also, if you're loaded with money or frequent flyer miles, many families willing to adopt could use the help. That way, you'd get the joy of participating in God's care for the orphan without the sleepless nights and strep throat and potty-training.

6. Senior Socializing

Many people living in nursing homes or assisted care facilities are starving for the company of a visitor. Some of these might be more than willing to skip Bingo and wheelchair aerobics and competitive crossword puzzles for a Saturday morning or Sunday afternoon spent chatting with you. If you've got forty-five free minutes a week, you can minister the real presence of Jesus to someone who is lonely.

The possibilities are endless. If you're an introvert, know that God has great plans for you to minister to a world in need as you employ your unique gifts. Be confident that you are entirely equipped to do whatever fresh thing it is that God has in store for you. The world waits for the particular gifts you bring.

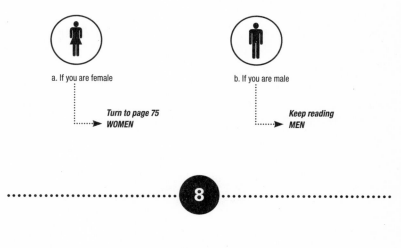

a. If you are female

Turn to page 75
WOMEN

b. If you are male

Keep reading
MEN

8

MEN

The Drum Major Instinct

SAYING SOMETHING MEANINGFUL about gender biologically, as it relates to puberty or reproduction, is no big deal. There's no getting around the fact that the bodies of women and men have been created differently. No woman is inseminating anyone, and no one who was born male is carrying offspring around inside their persons.

Saying anything meaningful about gender as it relates to *discipleship* begins to get dicey. As well it should.

Since there are no reproductive organs involved, there's no good reason that the ways our eyes and ears see and hear God and the ways our arms and legs respond to God would be different at all. Thankfully, since we're exploring what it means to engage with a world in need by entering into relationship with folks we don't yet know very well, there's no good reason that reproductive organs really *need* to be involved.

What *is* legit, I think, and certainly more helpful as we think about discipleship, is to notice the ways that women and men have been formed in our culture. As we recognize the ways our culture has shaped us, we can look at how those influences do, or don't, equip us to follow Jesus. Ted Smith, who teaches at Vanderbilt University, observes that women and men are formed in a wide variety of different ways in contemporary culture. The roles for each gender are multiple and they often overlap. And then people play upon those roles in an infinite variety of ways. That said, gender roles clump together in ways that allow for some loose, fallible generalities. Smith says, "I think we form men in ways that give many men large needs for differentiation, for setting ourselves apart as *better-than*. This can take many forms: athletic, financial and the everyday stuff of talking smack in a bar or academic seminar room."

I really think he's on to something. The *better-than* he's describing, familiar to many, is anti-Christian. It is contrary to the pattern of self-giving love that God established in Jesus. And if that's the way our culture, and many others, have *formed* men, then as we think about engaging a world in need, we need to figure out how discipleship will *transform* them.[1]

---

[1]Yes, yes, women too. Men, though, have borne the brunt of it.

TWO EAGER BROTHERS

Two of Jesus' friends who were quite interested in being set apart were James and John. Specifically, they wanted to be elevated to his left and right hand. Jesus' response—whether he'll choose to ignore them or shame them or promote them—informs what it looks like for Christian men to follow Jesus today.

Martin Luther King Jr. unpacks Jesus' response to brothers James and John in his 1968 sermon "The Drum Major Instinct," adapted from a 1952 homily by J. Wallace Hamilton. It was my friend Ted, the one from Vanderbilt, who tipped me off to this helpful unpacking. Though King is not analyzing gender, I do believe the shoe fits. So let's try it on.

King identifies with James and John, and he welcomes others to do so as well. "We have some of the same James and John qualities," King explains. "And there is deep down within all of us an instinct. It's a kind of drum major instinct—a desire to be out front, a desire to lead the parade, a desire to be first." Whether or not he speaks for all of us on this one is debatable. He probably does speak for a lot of men, however, and most certainly speaks for himself.

After the brothers have asked Jesus to save them front-row seats right next to his, King summarizes Jesus' response to the brothers: "[Jesus] said in substance, 'Oh, I see, you want to be first. You want to be great. You want to be important. You want to be significant. Well, you ought to be. If you're going to be my disciple, you must be.'"

As you can tell, it's going to be pretty important that you stay with this argument to the end. This would be a bad moment to stop reading.

Because the other disciples get a little cranky when they catch wind of it, Jesus addresses all twelve of the friends. Gathering everyone together, Jesus teaches, "You know that among the Gentiles those whom they recognize as their rulers lord it over them, and their great ones are tyrants over them" (Mark 10:42). Of course they know. Each one of them knows that this is how authority and leadership and power work in a patriarchal society. I also have to believe that a few others probably secretly want Jesus to choose them as corulers. Possibly ten others.

After deferring HR issues like promotions to another department, Jesus turns it all upside down with one of those now-churchified injunctions that can be so hard to hear with fresh ears: "Whoever wishes to become great among you must be your servant, and whoever wishes to be first among you must be slave of all" (Mark 10:43-44).

In case you missed that, like a ninety-eight-mile-per-hour fastball, King explains what just happened: "He reordered priorities. And he said, 'Yes, don't give up this instinct. It's a good instinct if you use it right. It's a good instinct if you don't distort it and pervert it. Don't give it up. Keep feeling the need for being important. Keep feeling the need for being first. But I want you to be first in love. I want you to be first in moral excellence. I want you to be first in generosity. That is what I want you to do.'"

Jesus redeems our natural and learned impulses by making them servants of a new order. Ted Smith paraphrases, "If you've got to be a drum major, be a drum major for justice." And I'd add, "Take whatever influence you've been granted—even when, and maybe especially when, it is a function of the ways you've been socialized into some gender role—and offer it in the service of Jesus and his inbreaking kingdom."

I do believe that was the witness of Jesus himself. It was also the witness of Dr. King. He was a drum major for justice. Can you imagine the damage that guy could have done being a drum major for retailing? Frightening.

In the kingdom industry, though—if I were being particularly crass—I'd put King in charge of advertising and marketing for all of Jesus' key initiatives. I can almost see now the large and small bumper stickers on all the manly Hummers and macho Harleys and peanut-oil-powered SUVs.

Achieve smallness.

Accomplish service.

Produce love.

Focus on the margins.

Work for peace.

Provide for the weak.

Be first in love.

If that sounds like someone you know, and you're racking your brain to remember just who it is, it may be Jesus. In Jesus, men and women see what it looks like to be truly human.

Aiden Enns, founder and editor of *Geez* magazine, adds, "I see in Jesus the ability to resist evil—which includes patriarchal structures, for example—to confront evil and to overcome evil, all with the conviction that love conquers all." That's the kind of *firstness* King is talking about. I believe the language Jesus uses for the same thing is *last*. I think you get the idea, though. Enns adds, "Suffering persecution for the sake of love and apparent weakness, while un-mannish in his day as it is in ours, is a way to be more fully human, especially for men."

What our culture would call un-mannish turns out—in Jesus— to be *exactly* mannish. Brothers, as you offer yourself to God's beloved ones who are poor and marginalized, be yourselves. As you resist the natural urge to set yourselves apart as better than another or others, you become the truly human selves you've been made to be. You also participate in freeing up others to be the ones they're made to be.

SALTY MEN

Recently I started to wonder what it looks like for *men*, in particular, to live and work and play among the world's most vulnerable populations. Specifically, I asked my friend Phileena, codirector of Word Made Flesh, about communities where women and children are being exploited by the commercial sex industry. Although I can see how men are already pretty . . . involved . . . in the commercial sex industry—driving it as clients, pimps and traffickers—I wondered what it would look like for men to exert a different type of *influence.*

Phileena paints a new Christian vision of godly men engaging the "johns" who are soliciting sex for underprivileged, oppressed and enslaved women. These men would model for the "johns" a new way of being in relationship with women and children. Reflecting on this possibility, she adds, "In every area of community and social engagement, godly men are needed to show up. Their example as a woman- and child-honoring human being speaks volumes on every level of society."

Can you catch that vision?

When Jesus told his followers to be salt and light in the world, salt didn't have anything to do with fries or popcorn. In the ancient world, salt was a preservative, so Jesus' admonition was for his disciples to be preserving agents in society. This is still the priestly function of those who, with their presence, preserve a society that operates according to kingdom values.

Men do this today as they model, in all kinds of ways, the relational fidelity that Jesus practiced.

Gender is one thing, and then *age* adds a whole new flavor to the mix.

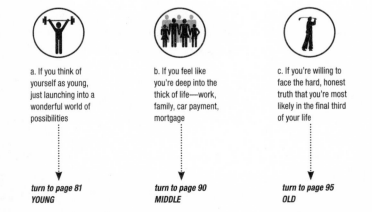

a. If you think of yourself as young, just launching into a wonderful world of possibilities

b. If you feel like you're deep into the thick of life—work, family, car payment, mortgage

c. If you're willing to face the hard, honest truth that you're most likely in the final third of your life

turn to page 81
YOUNG

turn to page 90
MIDDLE

turn to page 95
OLD

WOMEN

Salvaging a Holy Train Wreck

WHEN I HAD THE HAPPY FORTUNE of sharing breakfast with author and speaker Tony Campolo, I wanted to pick his brain. Specifically, I asked him if there is a particular way to inspire and equip women whose basic needs are met—women like me who read books like this—to use what we've got to make a difference in the world.

"Tell me this," he began, a devilish twinkle in his eye. "Who is it that *makes* the money?"

I looked at him blankly. This was clearly one of those questions where the teacher already knows the right answer and it's up to the student to read the teacher's mind.

I really hate these situations.

Then, with another twinkle, he proudly announced, "Men!"

I had not seen that coming. Because that was, like, *way* old school. That was *Leave It to Beaver* old school.

"Men make the money, and women spend it!" he continued with delight. He really said those words out loud.

My mind raced to make sense of how someone I respect so much could have just said something so ridiculous and sexist. Our conversation suddenly felt to me like a weird 1950s train wreck.

He continued to press on, demanding, "Who buys the groceries?"

I had just enough self-respect left to not parrot the answer I suspected he was fishing for.

"Women," he said, proudly. "And who buys the clothes for the family, for the children?" he continued to press.

It was not at all clear to me whether he knew that it was no longer 1950 or that every woman was not married with children. I'd let him wait a long time for this student to parrot the correct answer, and so simply shoved in another large mouthful of Raisin Bran.

"Women," he continued, gathering steam.

"Who decides where the family lives? Women!" he trumpeted.

I quickly scanned the perimeter of the breakfast table for any sane allies, because I really wanted some witnesses. Everyone else, however, was busy chatting in other directions.

Meanwhile, a thought slowly began to form in my mind: *What if he's not as wrong as I want him to be?* Obvious offense aside— which, like a needling big brother, is what I think he was aiming for all along—I began to wonder if he might actually be on to something. What he suggested might *possibly* be true for a hyper-traditional household in which the man, wearing wingtip shoes and grabbing his briefcase, leaves the house in the 'burbs each morning to earn the wages. In this reality, in which the hot-curler-using, lipstick-glossed, pearl-draped woman stays home to paint her nails and vacuum in stilettos—this woman who probably only exists in my mind—I could see how he might just be right. She probably *did* choose the neighborhood, buy the groceries, cook the food and clothe the children.

A WEE BIT SENSITIVE

Weirdly, sans the hair, lips, accessories, nails and housework, this is my own situation. Perhaps this is why I was feeling touchy. The home happens to be where I get a lot of my work done, and I do gather food and make sure my kids are wearing shoes when they leave the house. Usually. Of course, if we need the food to taste good, or the kids to look right, a consult with my husband is often requisite. But I can manage the basics. Most days.

So as all the rage chemicals that had been released in my brain started to dissipate, I could admit that women in these more traditional situations probably *do* have a fair bit of influence over the household's choice of neighborhood and food and clothes and other stuff.

Can you see where this is going?

I clearly wanted to be incensed about Tony's antiquated gender notions on behalf of the single women, and married ones, and divorced ones, and the working-in-an-office women and the working-from-home women. I even wanted to be furious on behalf of those of us who manage households and children and sippy cups and magazine subscriptions. But all Tony was really saying was that women in the most traditional circumstances have real power in a household. Using this single sentence would have been much more efficient, I believe, though it would not have achieved the blood-boiling impact. As the pieces started falling into place, my rage quickly shifted to intrigue. After all, if women in the most traditional circumstances have, as Tony suggested, more power than at first meets the eye—by virtue of their economic influence—then women who are *not* married and those who *are* working outside the home and those who *aren't* raising children most certainly do too. More, it seems.

Are you tracking with me?

THIS IS PRETTY BIG

I understand that it might be hard for some women to get really jazzed about this, because given the choice between all that great "influence" and the alternative—maybe popping open a beer, kicking up our feet and watching a football game—we'd prefer the latter. I get that.

This is big, though, women. This is very big.

Whether you're running a company or homeschooling your children or pursuing a graduate degree—or all of these at once,

God bless you—you might just possibly have a world of untapped influence that you've not yet even considered. Here, I'm thinking about the healthy ways women are often connected relationally to others, particularly those on the margins. Specifically, I'm thinking about the ways that women often have an acute peripheral perspective that holds the needs of the collective in view. And while there's a legitimate argument to be made that bearing the lion's share of cooking and shopping and clothing is a real bummer, there's also this fabulous possibility that, should this be your personal situation, you can use all that influence—and more!—to affect the world that God loves.

This new vision for the powerful impact women can and are having on society isn't nearly as old-fashioned as Tony made it sound. A feature in my city's local independent newspaper this week highlights feminists who are reclaiming the domestic sphere with an eye—and sometimes a green thumb—for justice. They're growing tomatoes and kneading dough and sewing clothes and making cheese. The *feminists*.

Yes, it still stinks that patriarchal societies have, for centuries, limited women's opportunities to speak and lead and achieve outside the home. It's totally wack, it's changing, and it needs to change more. But when the sinful debacle is reframed in terms of the influence that women *have* garnered in more traditional spheres, empowering them to use it as kingdom agents, it begins to smack of what God did through Jacob's son Joseph.

Although Joseph's brothers used their power to forcibly silence and subjugate him, God had something else in mind for Joseph. Talk about influencing a world in need! In the face of famine and despair, Joseph was God's chosen agent of redemption. When they realized this, Joseph's brothers crumbled into tears, threw themselves down on the ground and offered themselves as Joseph's slaves.

As a physically weaker little sister, six years younger than my large football-playing brother, I can tell you that it takes one healthy sibling to resist taking advantage of that sweet moment. But resisting any impulse to gloat, Joseph explains, "Even though you intended to do harm to me, God intended it for good, in order to preserve a numerous people, as he is doing today" (Genesis 50:20).

Women, can you claim that attitude? Can you own it?

It seems like Jesus did.

COVERT GYNO OPS

Not only do we women have influence to wield for evil or for good, we also can have access to opportunities that men may not.

A few years ago I was winding my way through an annoying interstate construction maze when I passed a stranded family with two parents and two toddlers. Their out-of-state car had broken down, and they were stuck in the median. The toddlers, as they are wont to do, were toddling. Dangerous, right? Especially when the father was trying to phone for help.

Because I was footloose and fancy-free that morning as I returned from preaching responsibilities, traveling without my own toddlers, I couldn't see any good reason not to stop for this family. But not for lack of trying. I tried to rationalize scooting past without a sideways glance but simply couldn't justify it. Add to all this rationalizing the fact that, since I'm seldom quick-witted enough to stop for a roadside need, I had to loop back. During the long loop, I prepped for my introduction.

I needed to establish myself as a responsible character. Mostly, I didn't want them to think I was a creepy roadside stalker who tries to kidnap portions of families. So as I slowed to a stop, I tried to perfect the pick-up line to sound as trustworthy as possible. If you've never tried to pick up someone in a bar *or* by the side of the road, these openers aren't as easy as you might think.

"Hi, I'm Margot. I'm a mother of two children. See, I've got the car seats to prove it. See them? Stretch marks too. Look, right here, under my shirt. I've been stranded on this very highway with my babies and it was the worst! They have to go potty, they get thirsty, they get hungry. Yuck. I do love those children of mine that I eventually got safely home. Did I mention that I'm totally not a creepy stalker?"

The trustworthy line was probably more terrifying than if I'd said nothing. But working my mad communication skills, I actually talked them into letting me take the mom and girls thirty miles away to my toy-strewn home, where the dad could fetch them later in a functional automobile.

This is my point: a man could *never* have gotten away with that. Hopefully, no desperate woman would drag her children into the car of a strange man. For some reason, one was willing to drag them into mine. Though I'd like to think it was my winning speech, more likely I have my gender to thank. Being women allows us access to people and places where men might not be welcome.

For better or for worse, it's the way our fallen world is. If a woman offers to watch another woman's wiggly kid in a bus station or at a park so the mom can use the restroom, she's thoughtful. If a man does it, he's feared to be a predator. Even if you just strike up a conversation on the street, others will be less guarded if you are a woman than if you are a man. If you happen to have a kid along with you, you're golden.

As we gently seek permission to share the lives of the weak and vulnerable, being a gender that for centuries has been treated as weak and vulnerable isn't necessarily the worst thing in the world. It may just be that your gender is the lubricating oil that will open creaky doors that are closed to men.

Once again, I'm entirely willing to acknowledge that I may be trying too hard to look on the bright side of this thing. I'll admit it's entirely possible. Yet meeting others in their weakness—*and* our own—was God's modus operandi in the person of Jesus. It was his unlikely eyeball-connecting, door-opening, life-changing superpower.

And if it was good enough for *him* . . .

Gender is one thing, and then age adds a whole new flavor to the mix.

a. If you think of yourself as young, just launching into a wonderful world of possibilities

b. If you feel like you're deep into the thick of life—work, family, car payment, mortgage

c. If you're willing to face the hard, honest truth that you're most likely in the final third of your life

**keep reading
YOUNG**

**turn to page 90
MIDDLE**

**turn to page 95
OLD**

· **10** ·

YOUNG

Chillin' with the Justice League

*T*HE WEEK I LEFT HOME in Illinois to attend Westmont College in California, my parents relocated to the Los Angeles area so that my stepdad could join an ophthalmology practice in Beverly Hills. Loading up the truck and heading west, we were kind of like the Beverly Hillbillies. Without Jethro. Or Granny. Or hay between our teeth. Or the sudden unexpected oil fortune.

Just north of my folks' home in Santa Monica is Malibu Beach, and to the south is the more edgy Venice Beach. Malibu is home to celebrities and other startlingly beautiful people who ride bicycles, play volleyball and surf. Venice is a brilliant tapestry of the barefoot, pierced, fire-eating, tie-dyed and tattooed. So I sort of felt more comfortable there than I did in Malibu.

Venice Beach was also home to many folks who did not have permanent homes. In fact, there was a makeshift tent community called "Justiceville" situated right where edgy Venice met upscale Santa Monica. And who would not want to live in a place called Justiceville? Tents, sleeping bags, shopping carts and clotheslines formed the outline of the village. Worn pieces of furniture positioned in the sand had created an outdoor living room. Faded by the sun, ragged chairs and sunken couches had become home to the adults and children who lived at the camp.

We quickly learned that the future of the tent community was a hot political issue in the area. Many of the homeowners who had paid a pretty penny for a picturesque view at the beach wanted to see the ragtag community expunged from the neighborhood. They feared an increase in crime as well as its natural corollary: decrease in property values. Advocates for those living at the beach, however, lobbied passionately for the community's right to remain. Both the indigenous members of the homeless community and their well-sheltered allies met regularly on the beach to strategize. I had read in the local paper that the gatherings were called "The Council of Justice." Raised on the animated Saturday morning exploits of Superman, Wonder Woman and the rest of the Justice League, I could not help but be a little curious.

During my first month of school, I took a Greyhound bus home for the weekend. On Saturday morning I was walking along the Venice boardwalk, searching for the perfect Guatemalan bracelet, when I noticed a large crowd gathered into a circle in the sand. Their fiery rhetoric wafted across the expansive beach toward the boardwalk. It was so fervent and compelling that I couldn't stay away.

I quietly slipped into the back of the group to eavesdrop on the strategizing. Although Justiceville was a two-hour drive from my school, I longed to be a part of what was happening there at the beach. Learning that one of the pressing needs of the advocacy group was to copy and distribute information, I took a fact sheet with me when I left. I had big plans to raise a little photocopying money for the cause by selling some of the tasteful-yet-never-worn clothes in my closet back at the dorm.

That night, the issue of the tent village came up at my parents' dinner table. When I thought of the folded leaflet in the back pocket of my purple tie-dye overalls, I didn't mention it. Only a fool advertises the fact that they've crossed enemy lines.

WHERE ARE ALL THE ADULTS?

Even at the time, I would have admitted that it's not so hard to cling to noble ideals—in the name of Jesus, even—when you're a young idealist who's not paying a mortgage or paying for utilities, a car or health insurance. I got that. Not for a moment did I think that I was any *better* than the generation beyond mine. I was just younger and poorer—though, clearly, still quite privileged.

As I looked around at other adults, I began to notice that following Jesus into a world in need seemed to get harder as age, income and the cares of the world began to press in. I saw young people living edgy lives of love, but I longed to see Christian adults who were pursuing a life of justice and care for the poor. Though reason would suggest otherwise, I couldn't help but wonder whether the radical Christ-driven life was really supposed to be age-specific to the eighteen- to twenty-nine-year-old crowd. That was certainly how it looked from my vantage point. Could the general religious idea be that the idealistic rookies did all the work so that the old-timers could get a rest? That just didn't seem right.

Sure, there was the apostle Paul. And Jesus. He was in his early thirties, for crying out loud. Ancient. Unfortunately, those guys were just too easy to segregate into a flannel-board ghetto that had no real bearing on contemporary living. What I most needed was a real live middle-aged hero who had forsaken luxury to live a radical life of care for the world in response to Jesus.

So, knowing it was a long shot, I kept my eyes open for that unlikely possibility.

AN UNSETTLING WELCOME

After my sophomore year of college, I traveled with other students to South Africa while Nelson Mandela was still imprisoned on Robben Island. There, we learned from folks who were leaders in the nation's movement toward racial reconciliation. As we prepared for our departure, our host reminded us that our own country still had racial wounds in need of healing. At his suggestion, I decided to engage with an urban community in the United States when I returned.

When I mentioned this to a friend back in Santa Barbara, she told me about a guy at our church who was recruiting volunteers to serve with Urban Promise in Camden, New Jersey. Ruben and I got together for lunch so he could tell me more about the summer camp for kids who live in Camden. Having risen to the venerable rank of Pathfinder of the Ridge Tribe during my sixth summer at Camp Miniwanca on the sparkling shores of Lake Michigan, I knew I'd have a lot to offer.

"So where's the camp?" I asked Ruben. I pictured something quaint in the Poconos where city kids from New Jersey could unwind in the summer.

"It's at a church in the neighborhood," he explained. Surely he meant that the bus to *go* to the camp in the Poconos picked kids up at a church in the neighborhood.

Seeing the confusion on my face, Ruben admitted, "Actually, we're it. We *are* the camp. We show up and put together a camp in the neighborhood."

I quickly deduced that there would be no jet-skiing or parasailing.

Ruben explained that these urban camps for kids had been started in Philadelphia by a guy named Tony Campolo. Because I already loved that incendiary author who said inflammatory things about what kinds of cars Christians should and should not be driving, I was in.

When I arrived, a student from nearby Eastern College picked me up at Penn Station in Philadelphia. We drove over the Ben Franklin Bridge and into Camden. The Puerto Rican neighborhood where we would be living was near the base of the bridge. The place looked like a war zone. Once-vital factories had been shut down. Any windows not covered with bars or boards had been broken out. Beautiful brick homes along the once prestigious "doctors and lawyers row" were boarded up. Graffiti memorialized the deaths of teenaged gang members. Young drug dealers, whose street names would soon be spray-painted onto the walls of infamy, lingered on street corners.

Later that evening, the full summer staff of over one hundred college students gathered at Rosedale Baptist Church in East Camden to begin our orientation. Following a picnic and volleyball, we gathered in the basement of the church. We sang some rousing praise choruses and a few funky Bible raps, and then Tony Campolo was introduced as our special inspirational speaker for the evening. After an afternoon of meeting fellow staff members and chatting about how we had ended up in Camden, I had already calculated that I was in the slim minority who had *not* come in response to one of Tony's passionate invitations at college convocations.

This guy was totally fired up. He loved Jesus. He loved the poor. He believed that the body of Christ had been called to make a difference in the lives of the poor whom Jesus loved.

Because I didn't remember ever seeing an older adult who loved the poor, I could not help but wonder, "Is this guy for real?" He struck me as being talented enough to be doing plenty of other things with his time if he ever tired of the "Jesus loves the poor" shtick. In front of my very eyes was the first old guy—fifty-five, to be exact—who I'd seen living a life of love for the poor in response to Jesus Christ.

The superhero I'd longed for was standing ten feet in front of me, wearing khaki pants and a blue dress shirt.

CURIOUS DEMOGRAPHICS AND AN UNLIKELY ROAD

It should not be this hard to find older adults who are living out God's passion for a world in need. But too often it is. Since I'm not a social scientist, I can't say for certain why young people are often more open to engaging with the ones God loves on the world's margins.

This doesn't stop me, of course, from throwing out some completely uneducated guesses. Maybe it's because there's already so much change in the first few decades of life that more change isn't a big deal for young folks. Or maybe young people are still vulnerable enough by proximity to, well, birth to see others in desperate need and know that it might just as easily be them—especially if they're not yet able to convince themselves that they've "earned" everything they have. Maybe they're more willing to see the imbalance of resources in the world and not be too terribly threatened by it because they don't yet have very many resources to lose. And maybe they're just naive enough to think they can make a difference in the world.

Thanks be to God.

The body of Christ desperately needs what young people offer.

In young adults, I see a great willingness to journey the Jesus Way. This narrow route is the one Robert Frost called "the road less traveled." I believe Jesus may also have made mention of this narrow road. It's next to a huge superhighway with gas stations and Walmarts and fast food joints at every exit. As you might expect, it can get pretty congested around the exit ramps.

Beyond all the restaurants and hotels and car washes, this skinny road has fewer amenities and more potholes. It also goes right through the bad part of town that most folks on the highway don't even know about. This suits most of them just fine.

There are noticeably fewer travelers on this narrow road. A fair percentage of them, though not all, are younger folks. Everyone who has chosen to travel the skinny road is there because they're willing to be less comfortable than they would be on the highway. They know that there will be bumps and bends and breakdowns. Some will lose air-conditioning. Some will have to get out of their vehicles and actually *walk*. The reason they're even there is because, when they noticed Jesus pulling off the highway, they took the risk of trailing right behind him.

This new way, of course, brings them face to face with all sorts of new folks. The indigenous ones who *live* on the skinny road— who can't afford cars—are there by no choice of their own. Since it's not legal to travel the highway on foot or by bicycle, they just don't have other options. Most folks who have a choice wouldn't choose to live on the thin road.

There are some earnest highway folks who are willing to leave the wide road for a bit to venture down the narrow road. They might even do it for a week of vacation or even an entire summer. In fact, some of the young folks who do even make plans to stay on the skinny road for the rest of their lives.

SIDETRACKED

Here's what happens, though: life happens. They'll set off down the thin road, get a few miles out and then discover that they'd really like something that's only available back near the exit. This happens all the time, right? A driver on vacation in a remote location will make a quick trip back to the highway for whatever it is they want or need—to the grocery store or barber shop or mall.

The longer you stay, though, the more business there is to do near the highway. The bank is there, to cash and deposit paychecks. There's high-speed Internet access, to transfer funds to pay off student loans. The car dealership is there, and the mechanic. The insurance sales office is there. The home furnishing showroom is there. The post office is there. The good parks for the kids are there. The church that so many people want to attend is there. Eventually it's just easier, and it just makes more sense, to live near the fat road.

I don't think it's coincidental that a lot of the folks who *choose* the skinny road are younger ones. They've simply not lived long enough to have had the life choked out of them—Jesus' words, not mine—by the cares of the world, the lure of wealth and the desire for other stuff (Mark 4:19). Though Jesus didn't say it explicitly, I'm pretty sure he was talking about rent checks, car repairs, dental insurance, flat-screen TVs and whatever flashy new device Apple will be releasing next month.

Young adults may be on the verge of getting carried away by all that stuff people keep locked in home safes: a mortgage for a single-family home, a marriage certificate, a life insurance policy, pay stubs from five-figure biweekly salary checks, keys to a vacation home and the warranty for kiddie car seats. Though none of those necessarily *preclude* traveling on the notoriously unpredictable skinny road, they can make the already unlikely journey even less likely. Much less likely.

What this means is that young people—who for most of their lives have lived on the family dime and are just now beginning to earn a buck—are particularly well-suited to navigating the skinny road. Though there are exceptions, many young folks are not yet bound to the fat road, like an unswerving trolley car, by all that other stuff.

My sincere hope is that, should you find yourself in this position, you can put having no stock options, life partner or vacation home into some Christian perspective. If you are young, or young at heart, without a lot of that stuff, you're much freer to venture down the skinny road, to find out where it leads, and to enjoy the good company of Jesus and his friends along the way.

The body of Christ is blessed by you and your willingness to follow after Jesus.

BENEFITS OF YOUTH YOU WON'T FIND ON MTV

In the letter Paul wrote to encourage the young evangelist Timothy, he said, "Don't let anyone put you down because you're young" (1 Timothy 4:12 *The Message*). I'm pretty sure he said that because, if we're being honest, old folks often *do* look down on those who are young. Cautious, they think young people can be too impulsive. Wisened, they think young folks are too idealistic. Sophisticated, they claim young people are too literal. Rational, they think young people can be too easily moved by their emotions and experiences. Sometimes hardened, they think young folks are too soft-hearted.

I may be mistaken, but I'm pretty sure the old folks' descriptors for young people are also true of both Jesus and his most committed disciples. Responding to the Father's lead *is* spontaneous. Jesus' teachings, at times, *do* smack of idealism. His followers, if you notice, *do* take his words literally, and—God willing—their hearts are moved, in faith, to respond.

Paul continues to exhort Timothy, "Teach believers with your life: by word, by demeanor, by love, by faith, by integrity" (1 Timothy 4:12 *The Message*). With the Lord's help, may the rest of us be moved by your example.

a. If you have plans to be a middle-aged or older adult someday—and I certainly hope you do—you'll want to be prepared.

Move right on to MIDDLE.

b. If you've simply got to move ahead to whatever is next,

turn to page 101, the last page of OLD, to find where to turn.

MIDDLE

When You're Well-Networked

IF YOU'RE NOT YOUNG ANYMORE, and aren't yet old, you might just be a middler.

How do you know for sure if you're a middler? If it stings when the liquor store cashier doesn't ask to see your ID, and if it absolutely burns when, on Senior Discount Tuesday, the one at T.J.Maxx *does* ask to see it: welcome to the club.

A lot of us middlers find ourselves bound to the lives we lead by mortgages and car payments and credit card debt and school tuition and therapy bills. Many of us are committed and overcommitted at our schools, our jobs and our churches. The technology and other modern conveniences at our fingertips leave us increasingly isolated. It's not exactly a recipe that lends itself to engaging with a world in need.

The clear risk of this life stage is that we'll become absorbed in our own busy lives to the neglect of those in need. If there's a gift that coincides with this season, though, it's that many of us have easy access to rich, rich resources through our social networks. Whether or not we've thought to tap them yet, these relationships have the potential to bless others.

For example, the perks that my husband and I receive simply by virtue of being resourced and well-connected are, frankly, ridiculous. Family members share their frequent flyer miles to jet us across the country. Gracious friends give us free tickets to college basketball games. Folks at church have given us needed clothing and furniture. One generous family member gave us an SUV.

An SUV.

This is all I'm saying.

If you're someone with a rich web of work networks and church networks and community networks and neighborhood listservs and family networks and alma mater networks, you have access to precious, useful kingdom resources.

HOOKED UP

In fact, during this season of life, you're probably as well-connected as you'll ever be.

As a child, I remember arguing with my brother over which one of us knew more people. I lost, because no ten-year-old will ever hold a candle to a sixteen-year-old. As we graduate from children's Sunday school, as we move into larger schools, as we have more opportunities, as we join sports leagues, as we add degrees and internships to our resumé, as we enter the working world—well, our opportunities to know others grow.

As we move into the later years of our lives, though, there will once again be a diminishing rate of return on our relationships. Should you live long enough, the number of relationships charted across the course of your life will probably look like a bell-shaped curve. My grandfather, Roland Selke, has poured his life out for others. Today, as he begins his ninety-seventh year on the planet, he does so without the friendship of so many people he shared his life with. Today his parents, two of his siblings and his closest friends are all gone.

What I'd love for you as a middler to recognize is that the many social networks that keep you busy at church, pressed at work and time-wasting on Facebook are incredibly valuable as we dream about influencing a world in need. In this season of life you have the amazing opportunity to bless those who don't have access to the same social resources. If you've got them, as I suspect you do, it's possible you haven't fully thought through how you can *use* them.

When I was brand new to the city of Durham and got an ear infection, it was no big deal for a woman at our church to quickly squeeze me in for an appointment with her doctor-husband. A few years later, when I was turning left at a green light and had an unfortunate run-in with a motorcyclist, an attorney-friend helped us figure out how to—legally—minimize the impact the accident would have on our car insurance premiums. (Should you be concerned about the motorcyclist, I'm happy to report that as he was tumbling to the pavement, he was well enough to flip me the bird. So that's a good sign.) Last week, when my son's foot was hurting, I emailed a friend who is a pediatric nurse and who was able to help us get a better handle on what was happening. This week my husband's brother is helping us figure out what type of life insurance we do or do not need.

STEWARDING YOUR NETWORK

On most days, I don't give a thought to the utility of these relationships. Spending time among folks who live in poverty and who do not have access to these kinds of resources was what caused me to recognize them. In communities afflicted by poverty, there's no successful businessman brother-in-law. There's no doctor living one block down. There aren't resourced parents to help with the mortgage when unemployment strikes. There's no older sibling who has been to college. Those living in poverty not only lack what they need to survive and thrive from day to day; they lack access to social resources.

Children living in poverty die from infections that a quick checkup and three dollars worth of antibiotics could cure. Immigrants who don't speak English and who have a minor car accident most likely don't have friends, locally, who are in a position to minimize their financial burden. Folks who haven't fallen in with educated friends who are nurses don't have convenient access to the most basic diagnostic medical assessments. For free. Those who don't have relatives or friends in financial services will more easily buy and borrow stuff they don't need and miss out on the stuff they really do need. The poor simply do not have access to the natural social networks that many of us take for granted. Most don't even have access to the artificial ones available to those of us who have learned how to leverage the power of the Internet.

Resourced reader, I'm not trying to make you feel guilty. I simply want to open your eyes to the rich untapped potential in these networks. I also want to persuade you to utilize them for kingdom good. And yes, I realize how troubling this "let me share my rich resources with those in need" can sound. And be. It's certainly not the answer to every problem. If you're in relationship with friends who need what you've got, though, it just might be *an* answer.

You utilize your networks for good when you use your influence to connect those in need of resources with those willing to share theirs. You do it when you phone a friend who's an attorney to help a fearful family whose son was just charged with a crime he didn't commit. You use your networks for good when your Facebook post about a winter coat drive garners six warm jackets for kids in need. You do this when you coerce—I mean *persuade*—a med-student friend into serving alongside Haitian doctors on a medical mission trip. You do it when your Twitter post for empty pill bottles to send to Haiti with the med student rounds up needed resources for an indigenous doctor there. You steward your network of relationships when you persuade thirty-two new folks to be tested as bone-marrow donors and one turns out to be a life-saving match. These possibilities only scratch the surface of what is possible when your rich web of relationships is utilized for kingdom service.

I'm not advocating using people. I'm advocating spending whatever social capital you've been saving up so that instead of begging your friends and acquaintances to cast an online vote for your funniest feline home video, you can bless those in need. I'm advocating employing your energies so that people you know with resources are allowed the privilege of sharing them in ways that change lives and hearts.

AMAZING SHARERS

I see this happening around me in beautiful ways.

Last summer, when my friend Suzanne's daughter attended a horseback-riding camp, she learned that several scholarships to attend the camp had gone unused because no qualified applicants applied for them. The following summer Suzanne did the legwork, through a sister church in a less affluent neighborhood, to find children who'd enjoy the camp. She helped them with the application process and served as a point person to help meet the girls' needs for lunch and transportation.

In a school district in which admission to top-notch public magnet schools is conducted through a random lottery, families without computers at home and without quick access to information about application procedures are at a distinct disadvantage. In one underprivileged neighborhood, just walking distance from one of these great schools, one couple went door to door distributing flyers with clear instructions about the application process and important deadlines.

As you work some kingdom magic, do it with humility—if possible, with invisibility. A friend of mine coaches a team of soccer players from an urban neighborhood. Seeing the inherent potential in one, my friend wanted to sponsor fifteen-year-old Derek to attend a weeklong Christian soccer camp. Though my friend was well-connected and close to the director of the camp, there was no reason that he needed to be the superhero who swooped in and wrote a big fat check for Derek to attend the camp. Instead, my friend presented the opportunity, along with the financial resources, to the pastor of Derek's church. Then someone from the church visited Derek's mom and let her know that the church wanted to make the opportunity available to him. That, right there, is kingdom genius.

Sadly, it reminds me about the times that I've shared money or opportunities with neighbors in need when, with a little creativity, I could have done the same deeds in ways that would not have been associated with me. Ugh. This whole business is a learning process.

Like any other kingdom resource with which you've been entrusted, your privilege and social networks are meant to be a blessing to others. So begin to dream.

a. If you have plans to one day be an older adult—and I certainly hope you do—you'll want to be prepared.

Move right on to OLD.

b. If time is short and you've simply got to move ahead to whatever's next,

turn to page 101, the last page of OLD, to find where to turn next.

12

OLD

Goodbye La-Z-Boy, Hello World

IF YOU'RE OLD—AND YES, I am too weak-spined to define *old*— then, uh, you've lived a little.

Fair?

You have. Whether today you're feeling pretty old at fifty-nine years of age, or whether you're undeniably and unregrettably old at ninety-four, you've still got some life under your belt. You've spent a good part of your life doing what you were expected to do, what you had to do and even—for some—what you wanted to do.

And now it's finally time for . . . drumroll, please . . . doing what you were *made* to do.

The bad news is: it ain't golf, and it ain't professional shopping. The good news is: it ain't golf, and it ain't professional shopping. Instead, you were made to engage with a world in need.

AN ANTI-RECLINERIST

Pat and Sherwin Crumley, both sixty-five, serve as teachers at a school for kids of missionary parents in Kijabe, Kenya. It's certainly not where they expected to be in their seventh decades. Married right after college, Pat taught English in Denver public schools for twenty-five years, and Sherwin served as a music pastor. For years, they'd thought of missions only as a dream.

Several years back, when a friend implored Pat to come to Kijabe to teach English for a year, the couple each took leave of their jobs for one year to go. They returned to their regular lives, but then decided to go back to serve another year. And then another. They fell in love with Africa and in being a part of what God is doing there. Pat emailed from Africa recently, "We count it such a privilege to be able to serve the Lord here."

By serving and loving students, the Crumleys' ministry frees other families to serve alongside Africans in other ways. Throughout the continent, the parents of these students run orphanages, serve as doctors, teach agriculture and start churches. "The kids here are amazing!" Pat adds. "In Denver my students were concerned about their cell phones, their girlfriends, their cars and their jobs, so they could pay for their phones, girlfriends and cars." Of her students in Kijabe she brags, "They know what's important in life."

Pat has a special heart for older adults like herself and her husband, hoping that others will get on board with God's mission to the world. "We believe in our hearts that everybody has a window of time, usually between ages fifty-five and seventy or so, where they can make a choice. They can sit in front of their TV in their recliners, *or* they can ask God for a place to serve." While I'm too much of a scaredy cat to say that crazy stuff myself, I do believe Pat has earned the right.

Pat is aware that not everyone will be called to Africa. She's quick to point out, "We know it's not where you are that's important, but what you are doing." I suspect that the Crumleys' *doing* is opening up a world of possibilities for other older adults to serve both at home and abroad.

This isn't to say that what Pat and Sherwin have chosen is easy. Right now their daughter is preparing to welcome her fourth child. Pat explains, "We want to follow God, and we know for sure that he called us here. But we want to be intentional grandparents as well. That's the tension." It's a holy tension that many older adults who are listening for Jesus' leading are going to have to grapple with. I pray that more and more of us will.

GOLF AND RED HATS

If Pat's enthusiastic message about serving as God's agents in the world is coming as news to you, it's because it's not getting any airtime on the radio and it isn't splattered on billboards along the road to the beach like those ads for luxurious retirement communities.

The messages about aging in our culture communicate something very different. We hear that getting older is all about finally getting what you deserve. You've done your part, you've paid your taxes, you've served on church committees and now, at last, you've turned over the reins. It's time to collect Social Security, receive your pension, travel and find a good living situation where the people your age aren't too decrepit yet. If you have grandchildren, you're supposed to buy them too many presents, load them up with sugar and then send them back home. Men are supposed to play as much golf as they can squeeze into a week, and women are supposed to shop and wear crazy red hats and drink tea. This is what our culture has painted as the good life. I wouldn't blame you if you're having difficulty picturing anything other than this for your waning years. It may be all you've seen.

Of course, the lives of many older adults will never be as carefree as the unfair caricature I've scribbled here. Not everyone has the freedom of leisure. Many older folks must continue to work as long as possible to provide for their families. Some seniors who are committed to raising grandchildren or caring for someone with special needs don't have money to travel. Many on a fixed income, struggling to make ends meet, don't have cash for the silly hats. (If you find yourself in a bind like this, turn to p. 155, CAREGIVER. It might feel like a better fit for your situation.)

Specifically here, I'm thinking about those older adults who have some . . . wiggle room. I'm thinking about those of you who have a degree of choice about where you live and how you spend your time and how you spend your money and how you use your influence.

There is simply no better reason, in older adulthood, to make your life all about yourself than there was when you were younger. (If you're a younger reader doing some sneak-reading right now, please make a mental "note to self" or have your iPhone make some kind of jangly noise in forty years to remind you of just this thing.) Rather, God has better plans for you. I am so convinced that God's purpose for you, in this age and stage, is to live love in a world in need.

Now, you don't necessarily need to swing an ax to cut firewood for the poor to use as fuel, or build wheelchair accessibility ramps or construct emergency shelters in Haiti (although this is exactly how my seventy-one-year-old father-in-law, Larry, gets his kicks). There is simply no shortage of ways that you can share your time and gifts and resources with the ones God loves.

CHANCES ARE HIGH THAT THIS ONE WON'T HAVE YOUR NAME ON IT

I want to share with you the story of a woman from Indiana that's a little bit inspirational. If you do read on, though, just promise me that the unlikelihood of you doing the same thing won't keep you from dreaming up your own signature brand of exercising compassion for those who suffer. Thank you, in advance, for complying.

Susan is sixty-six. She's white. She's got a master's degree. She's retired. She's married and a grandmother to eleven. Her parents are both in their midnineties. She lives in suburban Indianapolis, near her folks, and the three of them have stumbled into a very unlikely relationship.

It all began about four years ago. After a long morning of doctor appointments, Susan helped her parents from the car toward a local sandwich shop so that they could enjoy lunch together. Inside, a busboy noticed the trio carefully ambling across the parking lot. Rushing to the entrance, with a kind smile he held the door open for the slow-moving bunch. Eventually, this became the family's regular litany after each poking, prodding encounter with a cardiologist, psychologist, neurologist, dermatologist or podiatrist. The busboy would gently lead whichever wobbly parent Susan wasn't escorting into the restaurant.

The nametag pinned to the apron of their new friend read "De-Randa." Although his shyness, a stutter and a mumble made him a little hard to understand, Susan and her parents began to know and love their new friend. Born when his mother was just fourteen years old, DeRanda was raised by his grandparents in Chicago's infamous Cabrini Green housing project. Though his special edu-

cation teachers passed him from grade to grade, eventually award-
ing him a high school diploma, at thirty-two DeRanda still could
not read or write. On his meager salary, he was able to afford a
small, one-room apartment within walking distance of his job.
Without friends or nearby family, he lived alone, with only the
company of his television and computer. Knowing that DeRanda
had no spare money for bus fare, Susan and her parents would
often show up at the restaurant just as his shift was ending so that
they could give him a ride home.

As their friendship developed, Susan started giving him rides
wherever he needed to go. Her ninety-three-year-old mother would
receive and return DeRanda's warm, gentle hugs. Susan's ninety-
six-year-old father sat him down for a man-to-man talk about how
to handle oneself in the workplace. Susan's own children and
grandchildren began to know and love DeRanda. In a relatively
short time, he was sort of folded into the family.

One day, when Susan and her parents showed up at the sandwich shop, DeRanda wasn't at work. When Susan inquired with
his supervisors, they said that they'd been concerned because
the typically reliable employee hadn't shown up for days and
wasn't answering his phone. His coworkers had no idea where
he lived. Worried, Susan and her parents drove to DeRanda's
apartment. When they didn't find him there, they checked the
local hospital. Unfortunately, that's exactly where they found
DeRanda.

Not long afterward, DeRanda was diagnosed with mouth cancer. When he was no longer able to manage at home, Susan found
a nursing home just two blocks from her own home that would
care for him. She bought him needed clothing. She shuttled him
to chemotherapy and radiation treatments. She found him books
on tape at the local library. She held a hospital bucket when he
vomited.

To this day, she still does. And although DeRanda is still sick, he is no longer a kindhearted stranger. Now, he is kindhearted *family*. God's business is to put the lonely in families. Sometimes those families are ours.

YOU WERE MADE FOR THIS

To make it quite plain, God does not call *every* retiree to integrate a chronically ill, mentally disabled man into his or her nuclear family. (You should be so lucky.) God's desire, though, for those who suffer, is for them to experience loving kindness through human agents. I'm sure of it. Sometimes those are sixty-three-year-old hands. Sometimes they are ninety-three-year-old arms. Other times a ninety-six-year-old voice speaks to another as a precious son.

You were made for this thing. You were made to care for a world in need. This may mean extending regular kindness to someone at your nursing facility who is lonely. You may help a grandchild begin to sponsor and write to a child overseas. It might mean sharing your expendable financial resources with those in need. There is no limit to the ways you can participate in God's love for the world.

Thank you.

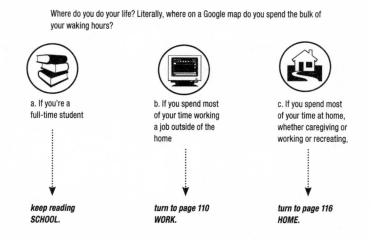

Where do you do your life? Literally, where on a Google map do you spend the bulk of your waking hours?

a. If you're a full-time student

b. If you spend most of your time working a job outside of the home

c. If you spend most of your time at home, whether caregiving or working or recreating,

keep reading SCHOOL.

turn to page 110 WORK.

turn to page 116 HOME.

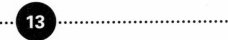

SCHOOL

Rule One Is "Love the Ones You're With"

COURTNEY PAULSON, a recent graduate of Wheaton College, spent the fall semester of her junior year studying in Ecuador. When she returned, the culture shock she knew would be coming hit her hard. Courtney explains, "I missed greeting everyone with a personal kiss of the cheek, sharing food communally, laughing, dancing and just celebrating life."

Gosh, who wouldn't?

Feeling low, Courtney stopped in at her community's local World Relief office, just a block from campus. She learned that they were looking for "friendship buddies" for a few Cuban families that had recently arrived in the United States. The next day, Courtney was escorted to a small apartment complex where she met her new friend, Lucia Boza. That would be the day that Lucia decisively waived the "fixed friendship-buddy hours" to welcome Courtney into her home and to her dinner table whenever she was able to come.

The two women began sharing their lives with one another. "I spent that semester constantly going back and forth between my small apartment and hers," Courtney explains. "I would help her read her mail, grocery shop, fill out important papers and learn to drive. She and her family would provide me with laughter, love and lots and lots of food." On the first birthday that Lucia spent in the States, Courtney decorated her house with streamers and balloons and insisted that she wear a crown all day long. Nothing says "Welcome to America" like behaving as if the world revolves around you. And, of course, Courtney got to share Lucia's tasty birthday flan. Most of the women's relationship was marked with joy and laughter—especially the day after Courtney took her dumpster diving when Lucia asked if they could return to "the garbage store."

After graduation, Courtney lived with Lucia's family for a month before leaving Illinois. She describes the time as one of the most meaningful experiences of her life. The last face she saw at the airport, at the conclusion of her college experience, was that of Lucia's husband, Courtney's Cuban dad.

NEVER BREAK RULE ONE

Students have rich opportunities, related to time and space and season, to build kingdom relationships. Whether your lips are fluent in Spanish or your hips are fluid in salsa matters less than your availability and willingness to live out the first rule of love for a world in need. Rule One, of course, is "Love the ones you're with." If, perchance, you did not know that was a rule, you are now officially responsible for the information. There may be a pop quiz.

If the ones you're with—students, professors, mentors, staff— are demographically indistinguishable from you, consider looking a little further. If you're lucky, your own local World Relief office will be located one block away. In lieu of that fortunate possibility, begin to develop a vision that notices those affiliated with your campus whose experiences are different from yours. Are there students on your campus who regularly dine alone? Have you gotten to know any of the international students? Do you know the names of the folks who serve you your meals? Do you know the stories of the ones who clean your toilets and vacuum your carpets? Have you met their families? Often the marginalized ones that God loves are *with* us if we just open our eyes to recognize and know them.

WHY CHOOSING CLASSES IS HOLY BUSINESS

Next, use whatever freedom you have by choosing classes that will equip you to be an agent of Jesus' kingdom. Mouse-click through your school's course offerings looking for opportunities that will open your eyes, educate you about those who live on the margins and equip you to engage with them.

My husband and two of his siblings attended Clemson University in South Carolina. (Go Tigers!) One student organization there, Tigers for Tigers, is actively working to protect the dwindling populations of tigers in the wilderness from extinction. When a biological sciences professor and international student affairs director caught wind of the group, they developed a study-abroad course in India. My cool sister-in-law Kate participated in that grand adventure. On the trip, students experience firsthand the plight of the creatures God commanded us to steward. Look for classes that align with kingdom priorities.

Even among required classes, you can often find ones that will equip you for mission. The possibilities are boundless. Pursue environmental studies to learn how one nation's overconsumption affects the poor around the globe. Devour history with a special eye and ear for the experiences of those whose voices have too often been silenced. Study liberation theologies to discover how the poor have read and understood Scripture. Learn Spanish or Arabic to give you tools to build bridges across cultural divides. Take sociology to better understand how culture and education and economics and politics and geography mold people's lives. Take advantage of the amazing resources that are at your disposal, and prayerfully work to connect what you're learning to the planet God loves.

WHAT YOU WON'T GET FROM BOOKS

Third, it's possible—probable?—that as a student, you have some sweet freedom that affords you the opportunity to engage with places beyond your campus, like India, in a way that a lot of us don't. Many students take advantage of opportunities to serve crossculturally on summer breaks or during weeklong trips on spring break. Does your school offer opportunities for you to really know and serve and learn with those in need?

When I was in college, Urban Promise Ministries exposed me to the reality of a world in need. My experience there opened my eyes to the intimate presence and concern and power of a God who is real. During a very comfortable childhood, I simply hadn't experienced a palpable dependence upon God to provide my food, clothing or shelter. The moments in my young faith journey that shine the brightest are the rare ones in which I was deprived of the illusion of depending on my own resources. I experienced this as a teen when youth leaders at my church facilitated an event that simulated real hunger in a refugee camp. I understood it when they drove the vans each week that took us to Chicago's Lawndale neighborhood where we met precious children who were growing up in poverty. I knew vulnerability when a praying saint led my high school buddies and me in prayer for a friend anticipating surgery, with the palpable expectancy that God would heal her. I knew my own smallness when, while camping on the shores of Lake Michigan, my friends and I jumped to the conclusion that the inexplicable display of northern lights meant the world was ending. I simply had no idea about God's realness and nearness until I was at the end of my rope, having exhausted my own resources. This may be why those of us who haven't endured much material need often return from our experiences in developing countries amazed at the vibrancy and faithfulness of the Christians we've encountered there. Those who live with fewer illusions that they are in control of food and health and nature often have a much keener sense of God's provision than those of us who live with the illusion of control.

During my transition into sharing life with people of faith in

Camden's inner city, I experienced a bizarre spiritual shift, like Dorothy's famed transition from black-and-white Kansas to Technicolor Oz. Suddenly, what I had understood as the "gift" of not needing to depend on God for anything was exposed as a grey spiritual void. Conversely, the new reality of *needing* to depend on God for safety and provision felt like the Technicolor existence. In this retelling I'm cautious about the risk of glamorizing poverty. I simply note that in desperate situations, the reality of God's presence and power is often revealed. As I encountered women and men of faith who already understood what it was to depend upon God entirely, I had the privilege of seeing the ways in which God works and is revealed among those who trust him.

You can't get this stuff from books.

The bottom line is this: during your years of study, you will be shaped by *something*. For some, it will be a shiny-shoed Wall Street internship. For other students, it will be the opportunity to travel with an intercollegiate sports team. Still others will throw themselves into festive weekend social opportunities. A few will be shaped by encountering poverty up close and personal. If you're fortunate, you will.

AFTER THE GRAD CAP HAS BEEN TOSSED

I doubt it's coincidental that, when I was a student, some of the haze of comfort and consumerism cleared a bit when I lived with less. Like a woman living with dementia who, during an experimental drug trial, has crisp lucid moments, I not only saw my past differently, I looked into the future differently.

After a few summers in Camden, I'd begun to notice what happened to some of the other enthusiastic volunteers who left and returned to their own homes and schools and communities. I kept an eye on some of my older college friends. They would graduate and take a job. They might buy a new car. Some got married. While paying off school loans, they'd buy a house.

Then came the kids, the car seats, the minivans. By no particular decision to abandon their commitment to the poor, it gradually happened.

I feared it would happen to me.

The summer I graduated from college I was given the opportunity to address the summer volunteers at Urban Promise on the night before we all left the city to return home. Knowing how my eyes had been opened as I had transitioned *into* the city, I recognized the real possibility that they'd squint shut again when I left. I still keep a copy of the words I spoke that night. My historic address began, "What I am going to tell you is something that you must think of every day."

Today I can hear how it sounds a tad bit self-important.

"There is something alive in your heart today," I continued, "because of what your eyes have seen and your ears have heard. If you do not deliberately purpose to protect that sensitivity, that freshness, it will die."

Reading the nodding faces, I could see that my peers understood.

"You will lose your first love unless you are deliberate about keeping your sensitivity to the Spirit fresh. Every time your heart is moved—by a beggar on South Street, or a woman walking down Westfield Avenue who has been beaten, or someone at school who needs your time during finals week—every time your heart is moved that way, you have a choice. The choice is to respond in love or not to respond. But each time you turn your head and pretend not to see, your heart will be a little harder in the future."

Okay, so I was a little melodramatic. Today, though, I am so thankful to have access to the prophetic words of a young, poor, passionate idealist.

PERILOUSLY COUNTERCULTURAL

Jesus warned folks about this very thing: that our hearts naturally end up where our stuff is. Idealistic students who are technically "young" and "poor" and "passionate" really do have a leg up on those of us further down the road who have become entrenched in stuff, debt and too many monthly bills. Own it. Nurture it.

With this in mind, prepare yourself for life after graduation. The nitty-gritty reality is that once you get your degree, and your first big job, and the car, and the rent or the mortgage contract, and maybe an additional family member or two, you'll be propelled, in all kinds of ways, *away* from those in need. I don't mean that you'll *intend* for that disappointing thing to happen, but without a concerted effort otherwise, it'll happen. Sorry to be so blunt, but you had to hear it from someone. It's just how the momentum of privilege works.

One of the ways to prevent it is by partnering *now* with friends who are also interested in resisting the pull of upward mobility that separates you from those who live with less. Covenant with a few friends who, like you, have tasted a better way, and find opportunities to support one another as you purpose to live counterculturally. Detail actual plans, in writing, that will tether you to God's reality and purposes. Be specific about where you live, how you live, how you give, etc. If living together doesn't feel like a realistic possibility, dig around a little and figure out why. If you're absolutely unable to share space and life together, pattern in monthly conference calls or weekends away to encourage one another. Because what you are attempting to do is perilously countercultural, you'll need the support.

You might also consider hooking up with an intentional Christian community in your area.[1] These are some great folks who can help steer you off the big, wide road that leads to Target and onto the narrow road that leads you toward the weak and small and forgotten. Feast on their wisdom by reading books like Shane Clai-

---

[1]To find a Christian community in your area, visit Community of Communities at www.communityofcommunities.info.

borne's *Irresistible Revolution* and other great stuff by Jonathan Wilson-Hartgrove and Chris Heuertz.

Last year Jenn graduated as a double major in English and Spanish from Eastern University in St. Davids, Pennsylvania. As a student, in conversation with some of her Mexican and Honduran friends on the college's housekeeping staff, Jenn had realized that a number of them were interested in improving their English. In conjunction with several professors, Jenn established an ESL class on campus, and now about seven students come each week to learn English.

When Jenn graduated she pounded the Philly pavement, searching for a job. And because seven somebody elses had their fourteen ears to the ground as well, today she is employed. Had her Honduran friend Carla not gone to bat for Jenn with a fabulous employer, she wouldn't be.

I mentioned this whole thing is a win, right?

In what sort of environment(s) do you spend most of your time?

  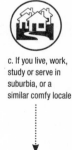

a. If you live, work, study or serve in an urban area

b. If you live, work, study or serve in a rural area

c. If you live, work, study or serve in suburbia, or a similar comfy locale

turn to page 121 URBAN

turn to *page 127 RURAL*

turn to page 132 SUBURBAN

WORK

Because It's About So Much
More Than a Paycheck

JUAN HAD BEEN AT HIS NEW JOB for three months when he stopped in the cafeteria at his office building to grab a soda from the vending machine. He struck up a conversation with one of the employees who served his lunch each day and who was on break. When Juan began to coordinate his daily caffeine craving with Kenneth's break time, the two men began to develop a friendship.

As they shared their lives, Juan learned that, with a new baby in the house, Kenneth and his wife now needed a bed for their two-year-old. Kenneth had been searching at garage sales and second-hand stores on the weekends, but after five weeks he hadn't come up with anything. Juan asked Kenneth if he could post the need on his church's listserv, and Kenneth agreed. The very next day Juan was able to hand Kenneth the name, phone number and address of Margie, an older woman in his church with an almost-new child's bed. Kenneth and his wife picked up the bed Saturday morning.

On Monday, Kenneth reported to Juan that his wife, typically quiet and reserved, had thrown her arms around the older woman. Noticing the sign on Kenneth's truck that advertised painting services, Margie ended up hiring Kenneth to paint the entire interior of her home, which she was preparing to sell. Win, win.

In the end, there wasn't anything particularly remarkable about a friendship between Juan and Kenneth. There was simply a willingness to engage, making a once-stranger into a not-stranger.

That's it.

And that's not so hard.

Whether you're a CEO of a Fortune 500 company or a greeter at Walmart, the ones with whom you can build relationships, the ones who are overlooked, might be right under your nose—vacuuming your floors, bossing you around or making your coffee.

EYEBALLING A LEADER

A number of years back I attended the Whitworth Institute for Ministry in Spokane, Washington. Because the keynote speaker was someone I really admired, I usually had my eyes tilted in his general direction. I didn't act creepy; I just sort of noticed how he operated. Though I didn't realize it at the time, I was learning how to do the work-slash-job of ministry that lay in my future.

At lunch, as this well-known scholar moved through the cafeteria line, I eyeballed him as he scanned the room for a spot to eat. Without making a big deal out of it, he looked around, surveyed the available options and approached a quiet young woman who was sitting alone. Asking if he could join her, he slid his tray across from hers and sat down. From that moment on, he was 100 percent engaged with the person in front of him.

The fact that this bigwig had no evident interest in socially profiting from anyone in the room was the most significant, lasting lesson I would take home from the conference. Although I learned it only because I was a stargazing celebrity-watcher myself, I think it's safe to say that I'm slightly less so now.

NEARNESS TO THE PEOPLE JESUS LOVES

Jesus-followers, in their God-given work, notice and seize the opportunity to embrace the person who'd just as easily be overlooked.

Too often, whatever our work may be, we choose to spend time with people who can do something for us. Whether or not we mean to, when we enter a room we're attracted to the ones who are, well, attractive. Though I wish it weren't so, statistics have shown that folks in churches who are less physically attractive receive less attention and care from staff and members than handsome and pretty ones. Whether one's attractiveness to others is determined by facial features, or race, or status, or fashion, or income, we're often naturally drawn to folks other than the ones toward whom Jesus so often moved.

Keep your eyes open for the folks in your own workplace—or clients, suppliers, those who serve you or those who are paid to open the door for you—to whom no one is flocking. Scan for those who are overlooked. Notice the ones who are less noticeable. In a word, keep an eye out for the ones Jesus would notice and welcome and engage.

A few years ago, my husband and I were delighted to be included in a weekend family celebration of one of the guys who worked construction on his job site. Kevin and his girlfriend had invited us to a birthday party for their one-year-old son. These were precious non-churchy folks we just wouldn't have had the opportunity to know otherwise. But the workplace, which offers this convenient, not-too-awkward access to folks we'd never bump into at church, had opened those doors wide open.

WHEN VOCATION AND AVOCATION OVERLAP

Besides connecting with people at work, you live into a kingdom way as you *do* your work with integrity and justice. You do it as you implement systems—even coffee and water cooler systems—that are just and sustainable. You do it as you refuse to cut corners—at the expense of another—in order to make a buck or save some time. You do it when you're willing to speak up for those on the margins who may be affected by the actions of your employer.

Your job is exactly the place where your faith and your love for a world in need take root.

My husband and I recently attended a dinner to mark the end of a green building project on which he'd worked as a project manager. The team had joined to celebrate the construction of condos, in a dense downtown neighborhood, that were built with sustainability in mind. Having gathered the team of dreamers and builders, one of the developers, who'd seen for the first time how many materials are often wasted in construction, pleaded with the builders to work toward eliminating waste in their industry. I don't know whether he is a Christian, but he was advocating for a very Christian stewardship of creation in the workplace.

When I think of one's work life being entirely saturated by faithfulness to Jesus, I also think about a pediatrician in the congregation where I worship. I've heard amazing stories from other folks about the impact this guy has had in the life of their children and their families. The ways that he makes himself available to families he serves is truly self-giving. With a passion for education, he offers his gift of teaching and expertise in medical ethics, both in our congregation and abroad. He takes time off of all this great "work" to serve in medical missions where his skills are so desperately needed. For him, work becomes exactly the place to engage with a world in need.

Frank, who grew up in a tough neighborhood and attended the school of hard knocks, now runs a successful local cleaning service. For several weeks in church, he heard the fervent prayers of a single mother for her son, Ray, who had dropped out of high school one semester shy of graduation. When a position on one of his crews opened up, Frank thought of this family. Knowing that Ray had had trouble with drugs in the past and that hiring him would be personally and professionally risky, Frank took time to weigh the possibility of offering Ray a job. Frank eventually decided that kingdom relationship—the opportunity to invest in this young man, teaching him to provide for himself—trumped his legitimate concerns. The influence afforded him by his avocation allowed Frank to practice kingdom economics.

There is no limit to the ways that Christian folks are influencing the world through their jobs. When I visited my sweet friend Courtney at Wheaton, she introduced me to two of her professors who have taken teaching to a whole new level. Sharon Coolidge is an English professor and her husband, Norm Ewert, teaches economics. Pouring themselves into the lives of students, they open up their house to students every week for a Thursday night dinner, at times hosting up to eighty people. They work closely with Wheaton's Human Needs and Global Resources (HNGR) program. Combined with classroom study, HNGR offers students six-month service-learning internships in the Global South to promote a commitment to confronting human needs through their lifestyle and vocational decisions. Supporting the fair-trade mission of Ten Thousand Villages, Sharon and Norm host an annual four-day sale, with goods trickling into their home for many weeks preceding it. I saw it with my own eyes. If you've got to shop, people, Ten Thousand Villages—which ensures a fair wage for workers—is the way to do it. The couple also visits the artisans overseas to nurture personal connections so they can then share authentic stories with customers, to promote better understanding. Courtney raves, "They built their house with scraps picked up on the street and dug their own septic tanks below the basement to collect rainwater to reuse in the house. They even experimented with an aquahydroponics system in their basement where fish waste provides the nutrients for hydroponically grown tomatoes." Fabulous, right?

Don't get me wrong: I'm sure great things happen in the English and econ classrooms too. The work that God has given this couple to do, however, flows out of the classroom and into the world. For Norm and Sharon, engaging with a world in need is part of that work. Among the lives they touch, it's contagious.

While some jobs like these might require a little creativity, other folks work in environments where this stuff just falls right into their laps. These are the ones who can't *not* be in relationship with those who are in need. There's no question that my friends who are home health nurses or hospice nurses do holy work. Social workers who shepherd children as they move through the state foster-care system build sacred relationships. With their faces and voices and bodies, these folks communicate to young people that they are worthy of love and attention and care and tenderness. This powerful kingdom reality is also reflected to God's beloved by those who work in restorative justice and among the mentally ill and with those who have various disabilities. For many, a kingdom vision of right relationship is fleshed out among the poor *while they're on the clock.*

Whether you work in an office or a church, a clinic or a school, a restaurant or an amusement park, you've been called to bless a world in need.

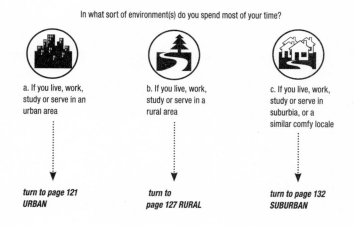

In what sort of environment(s) do you spend most of your time?

a. If you live, work, study or serve in an urban area

b. If you live, work, study or serve in a rural area

c. If you live, work, study or serve in suburbia, or a similar comfy locale

turn to page 121 URBAN

turn to page 127 RURAL

turn to page 132 SUBURBAN

·············· **15** ··············

HOME

Hospitality That Has Nothing to Do with Martha Stewart

EACH YEAR A NUMBER OF FOLKS from our congregation in Durham, North Carolina, take a weekend-long pilgrimage into the heart of the city. For several months participants prepare by meeting together, reading, learning more about the city and discussing. Then, from Friday to Sunday, these pilgrims listen to the local voices that aren't always heard. They hear from folks who fought for civil rights fifty years ago. They worship with one congregation in Spanish. They hear from a woman who hosts a prayer vigil at the site of every violent murder in the city.

Our Presbyterian congregation, whose adult membership is historically white, has a friendship with a local Baptist congregation that is historically black. Saturday evening the pilgrims meet at St. John's Missionary Baptist Church. As the evening ends, sisters and brothers from St. John's welcome mostly pale Presbyterians to lodge overnight in their homes. Some of the homes are located in the church's urban neighborhood, others are in a middle-class black neighborhood, and one house is in a fancy neighborhood in nearby Raleigh. Paired off, brand new acquaintances load up in cars and trek off together for the night.

This countercultural hospitality never ceases to boggle my mind. Every single year it happens again, and every single year I marvel at how right, and *rare*, it is.

This said, I do not mean to imply that the kingdom has come on earth as it is in heaven here in Durham, North Carolina. Though many of us long for more authentic relationships of trust and vulnerability, we more often bumble along in fits and starts. There's no question that we still have a long way to go together. But I am sure that every journey begins with one small step. One of our small steps just happens to be a sleepover party.

I find what's happening in the pilgrimage energizing because, when I mentally scroll back through my own experience, I can think of only a few opportunities in my life to either give or receive this kind of radical, crosscultural hospitality. I'd wager a bet that, like me, few of the most progressive folks I know have had regular opportunities to share meals and cars and pillows with those whose life experience is substantially different from their own. Go ahead; take a moment to do your own personal math. When your calculations are complete, I believe you will see my point. And if your figures prove me a fool, well then, praise God.

Too often, the people who share our homes, eat at our tables, and use our toilets are a fairly homogenous bunch. Typically they look like us, speak like us and act like us. This is particularly important to process if you're someone who, like me, spends the bulk of your week in or near your dwelling, as opposed to being out and about in a more traditional workplace or on a campus.

If this is you, and you're serious about building relationships across barriers, then you've got two options. The first is that you can walk out your front door and engage with the world outside. The second option is that you can invite the world past the threshold and into your home. Both have exciting kingdom possibilities.

MOVING OUT THE DOOR

The introvert in me loves to be at home. While I wish I were the kind of person who would choose bungee jumping in Bali or skydiving in São Paulo over painting on canvas in my hallway or sitting at my table beading a necklace with my daughter, it's simply not the case. Because I don't consider myself either fearful or lazy or boring, I'm pretty much okay with this. The reality, though, is that the odds of me naturally crossing paths with someone in need—a need bigger than not being able to find one's bead tweezers—is decidedly greater in Bali or São Paulo than it is in my dining room. The odds actually increase pretty dramatically just six feet outside my front door. So sometimes I need to leave home.

When those of us who live in comfortable circumstances leave home, we're one step closer to encountering the ones God loves who experience want. Often, being exposed to a world in need is as simple as walking someplace, like the store or bank, instead of driving. Liberated from the insulation of our cars, we have the opportunity to encounter folks who stand at bus stops. On the ground we cross paths with ones who *aren't* hurtling off in their SUVs to the store or bank, clutching a fistful of maxed-out credit cards. Leaving our homes gives us access to some of the folks we won't find inside of them.

A visit to an agency that already interfaces with those in need, like a local ministry or United Way, can also hook you up with a new friend who'd never in a gazillion years naturally end up on your front porch. Most nursing homes, with precious adults who are hungry for company, welcome volunteer visitors. Shelters and other urban ministries can schedule you to serve among their folks. Hospitals often have opportunities for willing volunteers. The point of all this is not to earn a merit badge. The big idea is for those of us who live naturally insulated lives to connect with the ones God loves and longs to touch.

INVITING OTHERS IN

The other way for you to engage with the world is to invite some of it into your home. That's right, I'm talking about hospitality. Don't worry: I don't mean the Martha Stewart kind. I certainly don't mean the kind that includes your pastor or your parents or in-laws or sister's kids. I'm talking about the kind of hospitality that transcends all the roadblocks that usually segregate us from anyone noticeably different from us.

When I invited my teenage friend DeCarlo to dinner, I was excited that my kids could spend time with him. Honestly, I thought it would be good for him and good for them. Too often children and teens who learn in special education classrooms can be neglected by their academically achieving peers. Not this guy! Whenever I meet teenagers who attend DeCarlo's high school and mention that I know DeCarlo, their faces light up. "We *love* DeCarlo!" they exclaim with delight. If their parents are around, *they* get a little giddy about him too.

Since I sometimes get overwhelmed if I have to coordinate more than one hot item, I hadn't attempted to cook anything too challenging the night DeCarlo joined us. But I was still a little harried after producing spaghetti and bread and salad. Then one child dropped a spoonful of red spaghetti sauce on the floor. Another was persistently irritating his sibling. The third was outraged about something else. This irksome stuff can rattle me at times. Though I was biting my lip so as not to say anything mean, I believe that my stress showed on my face.

DeCarlo took one look at me and knew something was wrong. I'm sure others in my family sensed the tension too, and hoped they could just ignore me until I returned from Planet Lunacy. Like I said, I hadn't yet yelled or raged or shamed anyone, but an avid student of people could recognize the stress. Calmly, like the world's best life coach, DeCarlo looked into my eyes and gently instructed, "Now, take a deep breath . . ."

What teenage boy even does that? Which ones gauge the emotional climate of a room, notice the stressed-out mother and gently help her get out of her stuck place? I tell you, I love this guy. Perhaps, like me, as you open your door to the Other, all your preconceived ideas about who will benefit most from the arrangement will fly right out the window.

Folks who would be blessed to get yanked into your living space—and who will bless you in the process—are everywhere. A new neighbor on your street may need a homey welcome. Or you might extend an invitation to Saturday pancake brunch to someone at work or church—someone completely unlikely, whose presence doesn't obviously benefit you. Jesus is a big practitioner of welcoming the ones who, for any variety of reasons, aren't able to return the favor. Maybe you could deepen a relationship with someone you've known who is now marginalized by transportation issues or disability. Think about a teen or adult who's socially awkward. I'll tell you who else doesn't get a lot of dinner invites: the families with eight kids and the ones with emotionally difficult kids and the ones raising a child or two with a challenging physical or intellectual disability. Right now just scrap whatever running mental list you have of witty and charming people you've always intended to invite over so they could fawn over your famous lasagna. Open your eyes for the most unlikely dinner guests you can imagine. I really think you might be surprised by how not-bad it is.

If you spend a lot of time at home, don't expect that a world in need will come banging at your door. More likely, you're either going to have to pass through it or open it up for the world to come in. Now you know.

In what sort of environment(s) do you spend most of your time?

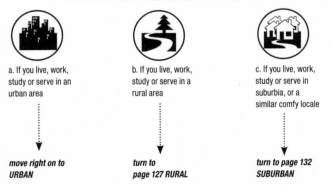

a. If you live, work, study or serve in an urban area

b. If you live, work, study or serve in a rural area

c. If you live, work, study or serve in suburbia, or a similar comfy locale

move right on to **URBAN**

turn to **page 127 RURAL**

turn to page 132 **SUBURBAN**

URBAN

You Have Hit the Jackpot!

THIRTY SECONDS AFTER bolting out the door for work, one of my housemates returned to announce, "There's a police car at the Smiths' house."

The Smiths lived six doors down from us. Stepping out onto the porch, I saw the flashing lights.

"Well, it's kind of hard to tell where it really is," I protested.

Then I heard it. I heard the angry shouts of Sheila, my neighbor. Six houses down. Because I didn't want to be a porch lurker, I slid back inside. When things cooled down, I would check in with my friend.

Because Sheila and I both lived in an urban neighborhood, our lives were bound, in very practical ways, by proximity. For anyone who lives or works or shops or studies or exercises in the more densely packed geographic space called a *city*, there's simply less chance to stay out of other people's business than in some other environments.

For worse or for better.

NEGOTIATING WITH THE ALMIGHTY

I was walking down the sidewalk in Camden, New Jersey, when I stumbled upon a pair of really sweet shoes. I don't mean that I saw them in a storefront window. I mean that they were resting neatly, side by side, in the middle of the sidewalk, sort of waiting for me.

They were white leather basketball shoes and almost new, and they were just my size. Since my own basketball shoes had already been converted into roller skates, I thought that maybe, just maybe, this pair that seemed to have fallen from the sky was meant for me. At twenty-one years of age, I could be very creative this way. I still can.

Scanning the area for the shoes' owner, I searched for someone who might be sitting on a park bench clipping their toenails or receiving some kind of public pedicure. There were no humans in sight. Bending to examine the shoes, I tugged at the tongue to discover that they were just my size.

Well I can't just leave them here, I reasoned. *Eventually it will rain or snow and they will be ruined. And it's pretty unlikely that the next size ten to walk down this sidewalk won't be completely skeeved out by the thought of previously worn shoes. Many people are. So it would be poor stewardship for me to just leave them here.* Those were my dutiful thoughts.

Aware that lots of folks needed shoes more desperately than I did, I made a quick little bargain with the Almighty. Though the only deal with a heavenly being that I knew about was Charlie Daniels Band's "The Devil Went Down to Georgia," where a guy wagers his own soul against a fiddle of gold, I pretty much understood how it worked. The human enters into an agreement with a higher spiritual power in which something is offered as collateral for something else.

Mine went something like this: "God who rains shoes down upon your beloved, and who probably wants me to have this cool pair, I humbly suggest an arrangement. I'll take these awesome shoes and wear them on my feet until you bring their rightful owner into my presence. Should the rightful shoe owner appear, I will gladly fork over the shoes in thy holy name. Or should anyone with a shoe deficit greater than my own enter the orbit of these shoes, I will gladly offer them as a good gift from you." That's pretty much how it went, my first pact with a celestial being.

I can hear how it sounds sort of . . . questionable. For the record, I don't make the "if you do something for me, I'll do something for you" game with God a frequent practice. For whatever reason, it just seemed like the right thing to do at the time.

NEON DISCIPLESHIP

I took home my divinely leased shoes and laced them up with a new pair of shoelaces, one neon pink and one neon yellow. Fall quickly turned to winter, and one day I was wearing the loaners while driving downtown. From my warm, cozy car I spotted a woman I knew named Elizabeth. Elizabeth lived on the streets, finding shelter where she could, and appeared to live with mental illness. She might have had a grown son someplace. Pushing a loaded shopping cart down a snowy, slushy sidewalk, Elizabeth had just turned into the McDonald's parking lot.

Immediately, I was aware that my moment had come. Though I'd secretly hoped that God might just find other warm shoes, without great laces, for everyone else on the planet before mine were required of me, it didn't go down that way. Because I have big feet, there wasn't even much of a chance that a woman whose build was so close to mine couldn't find a way to squeeze her feet into them. Grudgingly making a U-turn at the next light, I returned to the restaurant's parking lot and saw that Elizabeth had gone inside.

Hopping out of my car, I dodged snowdrifts and slush puddles so that I wouldn't be turning over cold, wet shoes. Even for someone who really needs shoes, that's simply not a pleasant gift. As I entered the warm building, I tried to look as normal as possible. Glancing down, I noticed that Elizabeth's feet, without socks, were exposed through her thin, holey sneakers. "Hi, Elizabeth," I began. "I'm Margot, and we met over at St. Paul's Church this summer. This is a weird question, but, what size shoes do you wear?"

Pausing to think, as if she hadn't had occasion to use that type of personal information in a long while, she answered, "Ten."

Of course she did.

I asked her if she'd like the shoes I was wearing. "It's a long story," I offered, to indicate that there was some entirely reasonable explanation for doing that weird awkward thing. Nodding, and without evident interest in hearing the long story I didn't want to tell anyway, she agreed. I slipped them off under the table, left them, said goodbye and walked toward the door. Creeping through the parking lot's wet, snowy slush, I tiptoed back to my car, cranked the floor heater and drove home in cold wet socks.

Now, I don't think there's anything laudable about giving away used clothing that wasn't even mine in the first place. I'm clear about that. What did fire me up, though, was the privilege it was to partner with God, as an active agent, in making real God's concern for the world.

URBAN JACKPOT

If you're serious about engaging with a world in need and you live or work or study or shop or recreate in an urban environment, you have hit the jackpot. The same sorts of needs exist in other places, of course, but in the city there's simply no escaping the reality of what it means to live in a broken world.

Though it might not sound like it at first, this really is good news.

Although I've lived in cities as an adult, I don't come from an urban environment. And because I've read the bad press about rappers and writers and other artists who act like they come from the street when they really grew up in a picturesque village like mine, I don't pretend like I do come from a city. Raised in the suburbs, I attended a respectable Presbyterian church, as did the core group of my friends. Our parents were teachers and scientists and pilots and attorneys and realtors and businesspeople. Most of my friends enjoyed intact nuclear families. Each of these families owned their own home with a spacious yard and a garage at the end of each driveway. The garages usually held two cars as well as a plentiful assortment of bicycles, skateboards, balls, lawn mowers, tools, grills and patio furniture. The most needy person I knew was a girl who lived in—wait for it—an *apartment*. It honestly felt a little scandalous to me, and sad, that she was deprived of the yard and garage and all the junk that garages hold.

In my community it was possible for a hurting family to preserve the image that they had it all together. Financial difficulty was kept private. Sexual indiscretions were covered up. Violence behind locked doors was hidden. Excessive drinking in the messy garages was mostly disguised. This sort of insulation is the weird privilege-slash-curse of those with resources.

When I moved to my first city, I quickly realized that those who live in the midst of urban poverty aren't afforded the same protections. More vulnerable, they don't have the luxury of hiding behind eye-catching landscaping or designer clothing. The inherent difficulty is not lost on me. No one wants to be forced into vulnerability. Ideally, being exposed, being vulnerable—which are essential for authentic relationship—are things we choose, not things that are forced upon us. For better or for worse, though, the needs of those who live in the city are often exposed.

A PREFERENTIAL OPTION FOR SHOULDER-RUBBING

Eric Jacobsen gets at some of this in *Sidewalks in the Kingdom: New Urbanism and the Christian Faith*. While hosting a play date, a mother whose family lived on a five-acre lot asked how the Jacobsens, who lived in a more urban area of Missoula, Montana, could stand living so close to their neighbors. Jacobsen expounds, "If we are inconvenienced or annoyed by living, working, and playing in the company of our fellow human beings, perhaps we need liberation from our selfishness and our willfulness rather than a massive home on a two-acre lot (soon to be surrounded by other massive homes on two-acre lots)."

Perhaps.

Jacobsen continues on to describe the benefits of this closer-knit living, working and playing:

> Living in closer proximity to our neighbors forces us to make compromises of our needs and wants—sometimes allowing us to learn the difference between the two. And as we navigate the delicate balance between our needs and those of our neighbors, we are presented with opportunities to take social risks and talk to our neighbors as we come up with mutually acceptable solutions. When we successfully negotiate these informal social contracts, what we gain—in addition to a satisfying solution—is a deeper and more honest relationship with those among whom we live.

That last part is why I think rubbing shoulders, as folks in urban environments do daily, has a lot going for it. Those deeper and more honest relationships sound almost Christian, right?

FATHER AND SON

Charles grew up in the Durham neighborhood where we both live today. While walking to the store, I had stopped to talk with him. As we chatted, neither one of us made reference to the drug bust that was happening on the corner just ten yards from us. Instead, we both kind of pretended like it wasn't happening.

During the conversation, I learned a little more about his life, his family. His face looked pained when he spoke of a wayward son. Before I tromped off toward the store, Charles finally disclosed that his son was one of the young men the cops had been interrogating, fifty feet away, as we spoke.

Authentic relationships are forged as lives overlap.

For worse or for better.

No matter *where* you live, your family situation is going to influence the way you engage with a world in need.

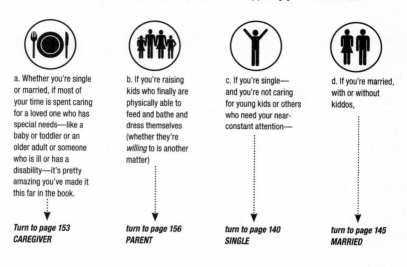

a. Whether you're single or married, if most of your time is spent caring for a loved one who has special needs—like a baby or toddler or an older adult or someone who is ill or has a disability—it's pretty amazing you've made it this far in the book.

**Turn to page 153
CAREGIVER**

b. If you're raising kids who finally are physically able to feed and bathe and dress themselves (whether they're *willing* to is another matter)

**turn to page 156
PARENT**

c. If you're single—and you're not caring for young kids or others who need your near-constant attention—

**turn to page 140
SINGLE**

d. If you're married, with or without kiddos,

**turn to page 145
MARRIED**

RURAL

Families Knowing Families

WHEN YOU LIVE IN A CITY, you see need up close and personal. With a dense concentration that cuts across socioeconomic brackets you could, quite literally, trip over your poorer neighbor. Late at night you might even have to step over her to get into your warm apartment. I hope you don't, but it's possible.

In the suburbs, need and weakness are more easily disguised. When porchless homes are accessed via attached garages, with the click of a remote, you don't really have to see either your thriving neighbor or your hurting one. Those who live in the suburbs, more so than in the city, can shut our eyes to a world in need. I hope you don't, but it's possible.

Rural life can be an interesting combo of these two. There's typically more space between homes, like in some suburbs. But, as it is in the city, folks can't help but know the needs of one another. There may not be someone curled up in the threshold of their home, but folks in rural communities learn about their neighbors' needs at church. They hear about them at the feed store. They catch wind of them at the hardware store. Teachers find out about them at school. Someone at the volunteer fire company puts the word out.

Just as discovering the needs of your rural neighbor happens fairly organically, responding to them does as well.

My father-in-law, who my children affectionately call LarryPa and who grew up in rural New York, explains, "In a small community, families know families." When families know families, you don't need to contact World Relief to learn whether anyone has a need for an infant car seat. When families know families, you don't make an anonymous donation of canned goods through a program at church to food-bank clients you'll never know. When families know families, the clothing you donate to others won't fail to be seen in school or church again. When families know families, engaging with a world in need looks a lot like sharing.

Though they didn't have an awful lot themselves, LarryPa's family practiced this kind of sharing. Grandma Vetter, who knit mittens and socks for the family, always seemed to have extras that found their way onto neighbors' cold hands and feet. Grandpa Vetter, who owned wagons and sleds, would take his team over to the next farm to move slabs—the wood left over after trees had been processed at the sawmill and that could be used as firewood. The boys would deliver used clothing, in need of just a little darning, to a neighbor in need. Locals who came to the farm for vegetables, milk or butter weren't turned away when they couldn't pay. Because they lived by a highway, even needy strangers would stop in looking for food or drink. At the Vetter farm, they received both.

LarryPa humbly explains that this type of sharing wasn't at all unilateral, however. "If there was ever a need in our family that people knew about, they'd be there."

In rural parts, loving your neighbor can be pretty personal.

WHEN COMMUNITY LOOKS . . . DIVERSE

Did I just make that type of community sound too Norman Rockwell? I fear I did.

Neighbors sharing with neighbors, though, is exactly what Jesus wants us to be about, provided that our working definition of *neighbor* matches his—culturally, ethnically and religiously. As for Rockwell, with the notable exceptions of his later work, the hues in his pigment palette over most of his career were pretty pale. He painted a lot of white folks playing baseball, bowing their heads in prayer and wearing Boy Scout uniforms. Certainly, if the pigment palette in your own particular rural area is decidedly light, then by all means go all Norman and love 'em the best you can.

Jesus' signature definition of *neighbor*, however, features a different cast of characters. The hero in Jesus' telling is a Samaritan, a guy who was the wrong race and wrong religion. If the community in which you live is more diverse, ethnically or culturally or religiously—like the one Jesus chose to tromp through when he dragged his friends through the unlikely Samaria—the neighbor Jesus invites you to love probably won't match the faces on your family Christmas card. I hope you already have a relationship with these neighbors who are different from you. If you don't, seize some creative new opportunities to build bridges toward them.

If immigrants work your land or live in your community, volunteer at—or start!—an English as a Second Language class. Or learn how you can improve the conditions of local immigrant farmworkers by learning more about the Coalition of Immokalee Workers.

Are there Native American sisters and brothers in your community? Take the time to learn more about the rich culture of First Nations peoples. Learn how you can best be a student—and friend!—of their culture.

If you belong to a "pale" church, develop a relationship with another nearby congregation that's predominantly not.

NO NEED FOR A PLAN

The Quaker Gap Baptist Church in King, North Carolina, found one creative way to love their transient rural neighbors. Folks in the church noticed that many of the employees at the local fair had medical needs but didn't have health insurance. Now, when the fair comes to town, Quaker Gap sets up a health clinic. Local doctors and dentists volunteer their time in the evenings on the days that the workers are setting up shop, so that these poorer folks can receive much-needed care.

Allow these relationships, those with neighbors in rural areas who are different from you, to move and transform you. Even if you can't quite anticipate what it might look like, expect these relationships to move you to some sort of action.

For instance, as you get to know your immigrant neighbor who labors in a field, you may find that your grocery-shopping decisions and fast food restaurant choices will be affected as you learn more about her working conditions.

As you get to know your Native American neighbor, you may discover that your own worship life is blessed by new possibilities in dance or prayer or language for God.

As you get to know neighbors who are culturally different than you—especially less affluent ones—you may find that your voting decisions at local, state and federal levels are influenced by these new relationships.

The Rural Organizing Project in Oregon is rallying rural voters who care about immigrant rights, economic justice, healthcare and other issues. In the effort to engage others, they act on their belief that sincere one-on-one communication between neighbors is the most effective way of making change. They're hosting local film screenings to raise consciousness and build relationships within communities. On telephones and on porches and at kitchen tables, members are creating awareness about the issues that matter.

Loving your neighbor doesn't have to start with any sort of systematic action plan like this. If you're the kind who likes a plan, though, here's one: *know* your neighbor. The world in need that God loves may be as close as the double-wide over the next hill.

No matter *where* you live, your family situation is going to influence the way you engage with a world in need.

a. Whether you're single or married, if most of your time is spent caring for a loved one who has special needs—like a baby or toddler or an older adult or someone who is ill or has a disability—it's pretty amazing you've made it this far in the book.

b. If you're raising kids who finally are physically able to feed and bathe and dress themselves (whether they're *willing* to is another matter)

c. If you're single— and you're not caring for young kids or others who need your near-constant attention—

d. If you're married, with or without kiddos,

Turn to page 153
CAREGIVER

turn to page 156
PARENT

turn to page 140
SINGLE

turn to page 145
MARRIED

SUBURBAN

What Mr. McFeely Doesn't Know
About Joe Poverty

HI, NEIGHBOR!"

That's how Mr. Rogers greeted me each morning when I was a kid. I was invited into his home. I saw where he hung his sweaters. I watched him tie his shoes and feed his fish. I knew how his kitchen was decorated. I knew that his mail carrier was the diligent and kindhearted Mr. McFeely. I knew what he wore when he left the house.

That's the stuff that neighbors in the suburbs, like friends of Fred Rogers, know.

It's the stuff that we should know about our own neighbors. Ideally, we know what time they leave the house and about when they return. We know when they're flooded with rain or piled under by snow. We know when they receive a visit from an ambulance, a fire truck or a police car. If we're worth our salt, we'll find out why. If we're not, we'll just gossip about our speculations. Sometimes, if we're the type to begin a recipe without making sure we have all the ingredients, we've discovered if our neighbor drinks skim or whole milk. We've found out if she eats cage-free eggs or caged ones. We've learned if he uses a manual can opener or a cool electric one. That's the stuff that neighbors know. Whether we live in middle- or upper-class neighborhoods, at the end of cul-de-sacs, in planned developments, or in gated communities, if we're in any sort of geographic proximity that allows us to see and hear them, we know something about how our neighbors live.

What we *don't* know about are the lives of the ones Jesus called our *neighbors* but who may not live in geographic proximity to us. If the ones who don't live near us are Jennifer Aniston or Tom Cruise, we can rely on the paparazzi who stalk them mercilessly and then make a buck for selling their private information to sleazy tabloids and television shows. So that we'll know what their lives are like.

When the ones who don't live near us are the poor, however, we lack the benefit of the illicitly gleaned insider info. No one is hunting down Joe Poverty to dig through his garbage or shoot a photo over his corrugated tin fence. We don't know what kinds of foods and drinks he gets with his government assistance. We don't know what he does when his car breaks down and he can't afford to have it fixed. We don't know what makes him laugh and what makes him cry. We don't know what games he plays with his kids. We don't know that stuff because we don't rub shoulders with him like we do with the neighbors who live where we live. And the celebs, of course.

UNILATERAL IGNORANCE

Unfortunately, this ignorance about our neighbors is often unilateral. Although the rich don't know how the poor live, the poor know exactly how the rich live. I learned this from a South African friend. Under the apartheid system, few white South Africans would venture into the black townships that bordered the cities in which they lived. Many had very little understanding of how black South Africans lived. The converse, though, was anything but true. Black South Africans knew *exactly* how white South Africans lived. They knew because black women folded the laundry and cooked the food and cared for the children of South Africa's affluent and not-so-affluent white families. Black men kept their gardens, built their roads, worked in their fields and mined their gold. Then, when these laborers were able to return to their own families, they listened to white voices on the radio and watched white faces on television and in movie theaters. Black South Africans knew exactly what "white life" was like.

This reality—folks on the bottom of the social hierarchy knowing intimately what life is like for those on top—takes an interesting twist in the 2009 film *Invictus*. In it, Morgan Freeman portrays former South African president Nelson Mandela. During the twenty-seven years that Mandela was incarcerated, he became a careful student of people. Rather than suffocating in anger at his oppressors, he spent his energies working to understand the hearts and minds of his white captors. After his release and eventual election to the presidency, this noticing went a long way toward his success. What is entirely endearing about the powerful leader was the interest he expressed in the lives of his staff. Across lines of race and class, he knew whose mother was ailing, whose child had a graduation and who went where on vacation. In this, he stepped down off the presidential pedestal to stand shoulder to shoulder with typical folks. He *loved* people by taking an interest in their lives.

To be clear, this hierarchical phenomenon is true of all kinds of cultures, not just ones with state-sanctioned segregation. It's certainly true of those who move in and under and through America's dominant culture. It is true today of the ones who clean our homes and manicure our lawns and bag our groceries and serve our food and watch sitcoms about lives that look more like ours than like theirs. The poor know how people with resources live. We're the ones that are clueless.

That said, however, anyone can take an interest in others the way that Mandela did. You can develop authentic relationships with the unlikely ones in your own orbit. Whether or not you happen to be the duly elected leader of an actual nation, think about how you might best get eye to eye and ear to ear with another. Take an interest in her. Ask about his family. Learn the names of her daughters. Find out what his mother cooked as he was growing up. Inquire about her work. Visit his church. Take her a meal after surgery. Share about your own family. Tell him about your hobbies. Let her know what makes you laugh. Share a meal.

Do the regular stuff.

Until now, far too many of us who live comfortably have been willing to just shrug our shoulders and concede that, whether we've been split by class or race or religion, "accidental" social apartheid is just the way things are. We accept the fact that we all just sort of randomly live in different places. So we take tins of cookies to a few neighbors on our street in December, experience some warm neighborly feelings and decide that we have loved our neighbors.

So—short of moving into a poor neighborhood or impoverished country—what's a suburbanite to do?

SEEING THE POOR

What you can do, and what *I* can do, is commit to initiating and sustaining relationships with folks who are poor. Traveling out of state for one week in the summer and meeting a very friendly local on a mission trip doesn't count. In case you thought it might. On the bright side, though, you probably won't need to do any traveling at all. Amy, a single mom of two, didn't.

Amy and her kids live in a gated community. The way these joints work is that when you pull up to the entrance, a uniformed guard calls the homeowner for permission to let you in. Then, once the owner gives it, he smiles at you as if he knew you were legit the whole time. Even if he was pretty leery at first because you drove such a bad car. In my experience, that's how it goes. So for my money, I couldn't imagine what it would look like for someone fancy who lived like this to be engaged with a world in need. I can be very shortsighted both when I'm being judged and when I'm being judgy. In this particular case, simultaneously.

When I asked Amy, who teaches art at a public middle school, what on earth it looks like for her to engage with a world in need, she didn't hesitate for a second. Immediately she spit out, "It means loving my students at school." Engaging with a world in need, for Amy, means loving the less privileged ones who pass through her door every day. Literally, she stands at the door as they enter, looks into their eyes, hugs them and lets them know that she's glad they're there.

"You're allowed to touch them?!?!" I asked in horror, afraid she might lose her job at any second. I didn't think that was allowed in schools anymore.

"Well, technically I'm not supposed to, but if they reach out to hug me . . ."

I got the picture.

As Amy spoke, the words of Jesus "For you always have the poor with you" took on a whole new meaning (Matthew 26:11). The popular meaning, I think, and the one that's really convenient, is to hear those words saying, "The poor are always going to be around, because, obviously, you can't really get rid of them. So why even try? Oh sure, throw a few dollars to charitable organizations, but we all sort of know it's not going to make a huge difference." Though we're not proud to admit it, that's the convenient but uninspiring takeaway for many of us.

I don't think I knew what Jesus was really saying until I heard Amy describing the way she deeply loves the students with whom she works. As Amy spoke, I began to suspect that Jesus had been saying something more like, "Even if you live in a gated community, if you're willing to open your eyes, you're going to finally *see* the poor who are right alongside you all the time."

Can you see how that's a different sort of proposition?

Amy really *sees* her students who are poor. I'll bet there are

Christian folks in her gated community who see and know the ones who manicure their lawns and clean their homes. Jesus is asking his followers to really pay attention to the worthwhile people who are already right in front of them.

My grandfather, whom we call Boompa, lives in a lovely retirement community. He treats those around him, who too often aren't even acknowledged, with dignity. From the widow living with mild dementia to the busboy who clears the dinner dishes, Boompa treats every individual as someone worth knowing and respecting.

When I visited him recently, my granddad introduced me to a teenager, who is black, who often serves meals to him and my grandmother in a common dining area. Though he might have justifiably coasted by with some eye contact and social pleasantries, he really *knew* this young woman. He knew her name. He knew her sister. He knew what her mom did for a living. He knew what colleges she was considering attending. He knew her hopes for the future.

I suspect you've seen how it more typically works: if an old white lady is being helped down the hallway by a black assistant, a friend cheerfully greets the resident while treating her helper, literally, as invisible. But that's not how my grandfather rolls. This ninety-seven-year-old man, who was poor as a boy and struggled to provide for his family during the Depression, really *sees* the precious person who is right in front of him.

THE POOR ARE WITH YOU

These invisible ones might just be students at the school where you work. They might mop floors at the Taco Bell near your office. They might stop by your church during the week asking the secretary for financial assistance. They might be hidden away at your local homeless shelter.

I'll tell you who else they are. They are refugees who are settling in your community, and around it, with the help of relief organizations. World Relief helped Khin emigrate from Burma five years ago. Khin, her husband and their three children were originally welcomed and hosted by a local church. When that assistance ended, they found a house they could rent. Khin's husband works at a nearby grocery store and, when she can find work, Khin is a housekeeper in local hotels.

Unfortunately, Khin was unable to keep working at her most recent job, where she was paid $3.20 per room. That's because when guests trashed their rooms, it could take up to forty minutes to clean one. You do the math.

When Denise, a mother from the middle school Khin's son attends, spotted Khin at the bus stop one day, she started up a conversation. When they passed several weeks later, Khin asked Denise for help. Pulling out a carefully folded piece of paper from her purse, Khin showed Denise an email address and the names of several local hotels. Though Khin's English was broken, Denise realized that someone had helped her get a free email address and that Khin needed help and the use of a computer to apply for jobs online.

As they began to work on it, Denise realized that Khin was illiterate, unable to navigate the simple steps of submitting a job application online. Together, though, the two women were able to submit Khin's application at several local hotels. And because Khin had a cell phone, she was able to receive and respond to calls from employers.

When we open our eyes, the poor are *with* us.

GENUINE NEIGHBORLINESS

Located in Chapel Hill, North Carolina, the Methodist congregation on Martin Luther King Jr. Boulevard is full of educated, attractive, successful people. I don't think that's the tagline on their Sunday bulletin, but it could be. Their church building is located on a fairly well-traveled road, and tucked in beside it is a trailer park. So you can sort of visualize the Volvos and Priuses and the occasional BMW that slide into the parking spaces adjacent to the trailer park.

At regular intervals throughout the year, a group of folks in the congregation go door to door visiting the seventy-five homes in the trailer park to find out how their neighbors are doing and what they might need. Some need groceries. One guy needed a water heater. People from the church next door, ones who simply took the time to meet their neighbors, got involved.

They're doing it!

These folks with manicured lawns and picket fences and the occasional gate-guard are doing it from right where they are.

No matter *where* you live, your family situation is going to influence the way you engage with a world in need.

a. Whether you're single or married, if most of your time is spent caring for a loved one who has special needs—like a baby or toddler or an older adult or someone who is ill or has a disability—it's pretty amazing you've made it this far in the book.

b. If you're raising kids who finally are physically able to feed and bathe and dress themselves (whether they're *willing* to is another matter)

c. If you're single— and you're not caring for young kids or others who need your near-constant attention—

d. If you're married, with or without kiddos,

Turn to page 153
CAREGIVER

turn to page 156
PARENT

turn to page 140
SINGLE

turn to page 145
MARRIED

SINGLE

Weird Kingdom Math

Note: this chapter is best suited for single people who aren't parenting small children or caring for other needy ones. If you are, do not pass go. Do not collect two hundred dollars. Turn directly to p. 155, CAREGIVER.

APRIL WAS IN HER LATE THIRTIES the first time she visited Haiti. A nurse by profession, April accepted a personal invitation to participate on a short-term mission trip with her church. As is true of so many who experience another culture, April returned from the trip a changed woman. What made April different from so many of the men and women and teens who return home all fired up about what God is doing in the world is that April *stayed* changed.

Deeply affected by the beauty and value and faithfulness of the Haitian people, April would never be the same again. In fact, she soon volunteered to organize and lead the church's next trip to Haiti. She used her connections in the medical field to gather supplies so desperately needed there. She developed ongoing relationships with Haitian leaders. She traveled regularly between her home in North Carolina and Haiti. With the support of their church family, April and her housemate, Sheila, constructed a hydroponic greenhouse in their North Carolina farmyard in order to learn how to implement sustainable food production technology that could be transferred to Haiti. Once they had worked out the kinks and had it running efficiently in North Carolina, the operations were replicated in Haiti. April went on to establish an organization that would support ministry in Haiti. In a word, April gave *herself*—time, talents and resources—to the work that God was doing in Haiti.

By my reckoning, April was able to give herself so freely because she was not married. Singleness provided this beautiful freedom in April's life—a gift of God—to respond, with abandon, to God's call to love and know and serve beside the people of Haiti. By her own reckoning, the complexity of singleness can't quite be packaged up so neatly and tied with a bow. By celebrating the gifts of a single woman, I don't at all mean to suggest that it can. I just don't want to miss what is possible when life is lived with kingdom vision.

While April was traveling, I was married and raising three small children. The only frequent trips I made were in my minivan to buy diapers. A myopic part of me envied my friend. When I stood back far enough to view the larger kingdom vision, though, I could only celebrate God's wonderful provision for Haiti, for April and for the kingdom.

ALL THE SINGLE LANGUAGE

As we dream about the particular ways in which a single person is uniquely suited to reach a world in need, I'd like to find better language. "Single" can make it sound like a person is alone, flying solo, tethered to nothing and no one. This, of course, is theologically troubling, because this beloved disciple *belongs* both to God and to the larger body of Christ. The only person this one does not belong to is one particular other human. In the absence of said designated cheerleader, the rest of the body is meant to celebrate the amazing but too often uncelebrated gifts that this person brings.

Younger single adults and older ones are gifts to the kingdom. Some relationships and work in faraway places and in nearby neighborhoods simply aren't easily accessed by someone who is married. Believe me, whether you're someone who longs to be married or someone who decidedly does not, I understand that getting to pull overnighters at a local homeless shelter or using your precious vacation time to travel to Haiti rather than Hawaii sounds less than inspiring. I don't at all mean to suggest that all the kingdom dirty work can be conveniently dumped into your lap, letting the rest of us off the hook. Yuck, right?

And yet, as followers of Jesus—married, single, widowed and divorced—we are all part of a pretty nutty upside-down kingdom. And if Jesus really does dwell among the poor, and if they are truly blessed by his nearness in a way that the affluent too often miss, then being in the kingdom trenches, doing God's dirty work, is actually a pretty fantastic place to be. After all, living among the poor was good enough for Jesus. As was singleness.

And there it is. I shamelessly played the Jesus card. Specifically, Jesus lived out—in a very particular way—a single-minded, single-hearted devotion to his Father as a "single" person. In Jesus we see what it is to be fully human, fully alive, fully beloved and fully engaged with the world God loves. Though I don't expect our culture to grasp the significance of this witness, I desperately hope that followers of Jesus do.

EXCITING POSSIBILITIES

Peek with me, for a moment, through a lens that celebrates the very specific ways that brothers and sisters who aren't married are giving themselves to the work of the kingdom.

When, at a highway rest stop, a man who doesn't have to rush home to care for kids pauses to help another man whose car has broken down, he imitates the Samaritan Jesus called good.

As a working woman in her midfifties cares for aging parents, she ministers to the most vulnerable among us.

When the unwed brother of a single mother pours his life into his niece, modeling for her the goodness of a faithful father, his love resonates with the Father's care for the orphan.

When a young single woman who has joined an intentional Christian community in the city tutors children in her neighborhood, she announces—embodies, even—good news for the poor.

When a man who is divorced shares a meal with local men who live outside in tents, he sees those who are too often overlooked.

When a recent college graduate—or a recently unemployed adult—invests a year as an intern with Mission Year, she learns how to love, and be loved by, the ones Jesus called "the least of these."

One single person who discovered the rich presence of Jesus among these "small" ones was Catholic priest and Harvard professor Henri Nouwen. After a successful career in the academy, Nouwen moved to Daybreak, a L'Arche community founded by Jean Vanier in Toronto, Canada, where women and men living with disabilities share their lives with mostly able-bodied friends. There, assistants like Nouwen feed, clothe, bathe, laugh, love and cry with the precious ones to whom they are bound as sisters and brothers in Christ. Initially the sights and sounds and smells Nouwen encountered there were unsettling. In becoming family to these beloved ones, though, Nouwen discovered that he encountered the presence of Jesus among the weak.

It's the plan.

The psalmist announces that the Lord puts the lonely into families (Psalm 68:6). Marriage is a designated way in which these families are created. They are also created, though, when a Harvard professor finds brothers and sisters among the poor who share the same Father. Family is birthed when a single woman welcomes into her home children who have been thrust into the foster-care system. Family is created when a Catholic man commits his life to God and to a brotherhood who are also purposing to be about

God's business in the world. Family is created when a working single woman befriends an elderly neighbor with cognitive impairments and without family. Kingdom family happens in the most unlikely places.

CAPTAIN JUSTICE TO THE RESCUE!

"Captain Justice!" I announced to the air, like I'd just seen him fly by in the sky.

"What?" my eleven-year-old asked, confused.

"He's a single guy who gave himself to the poor," I announced, as if she cared. Zoe knows I think about this kind of stuff all the time, but usually I'm kind enough to not bother her with it.

She does know who I mean. As a law student at North Carolina Central University, our groovy friend David spent a summer in Bolivia with International Justice Mission (IJM). Because IJM sounds so much like Superman's and Wonder Woman's umbrella organization, the Justice League, we simply could not *not* start calling him Captain Justice. In fact, I actually stitched him a pretty awesome supersuit before he left. It had a stretchy blue and red cape embroidered with a glittery gold "J." We also made him wear boys superhero Underoos *over* his pants and pull more underpants over his head, with two eye holes cut out, as a mask. Clearly, Captain Justice's most impressive superpower is being a *very* good sport.

Down in Bolivia, however, David more often dressed in stifling hot business attire. When he was trolling the streets with an informant, ducking down in the backseat of a car, David wasn't wearing the shiny Lycra cape. When those who traffic women and children finally went to trial, I can promise you he wasn't wearing a crazy costume like he did to humor us back in the States. When David participated in the liberation of captives God loves, reuniting families, this guy employed every social grace and kindness and energy and intelligence. Being single allowed him to be abroad for three months and serve the poor in a very particular way.

Isn't it a nutty premise? Single people becoming the critical seed of the kingdom family is counterintuitive. Yet single people who offer God their singleness have a precious, irreplaceable gift to share with the new family God is building.

Now that you can begin to imagine what it might look like to build relationships with those near you

turn to page 175
MINDFULNESS
to discover how to live
in right relationship
with the beloved poor
who are less visible

20

MARRIED

Oscar, Felix and Jesus

MY HUSBAND AND I ARE THE fiscal Odd Couple. Financially, I'm the sloppy version of Oscar and he's the more orderly and fiscally responsible Felix. Specifically, he makes most of the money, makes sure we give at least 10 percent, pays all the bills and tries to save a little bit. I mostly spend and give. Occasionally I'll make a buck.

This is why I always feel nervous before I talk to him about how we might be living a more radical life of love for the poor. This is how I was feeling last week before the following conversation.

Very casually, as if I might be asking what color socks he was planning to wear the next day, I calmly queried, "Could you live eating less meat than we do?"

Knowing I'd been sneak-reading some books on Sabbath economics, he countered loathingly, "Is this about *justice*?" The final word dripped with wicked disgust. He used the same tone one might employ if they were asking, "Is this about your numskulled insistence on browsing through porn magazines with the children at bedtime?" Really, he was that disgusted.

I know my beloved well enough to quickly recognize that this conversation was not going to go anywhere I might have hoped. Better to cut my losses, I figured, and try again later. When he was distracted. And possibly overmedicated. Maybe unconscious.

"Justice?!" I retorted indignantly. "Are you kidding me? I *hate* justice! Yuck, gross, blech. Stupid justice. Justice, shmustice. I was just randomly curious about how carnivorous you are at this particular moment in time."

Though I wanted that to end it, I could tell from his face that I wasn't going to get off the hook quite so easily. Both of us knew that it *was* about justice and that he was on the edge of blurting out, "When hell freezes over."

You know how crazy wild animals get when they're trapped in a corner? You know how they sort of bite and claw at the closest loving creature, even if that creature is trying to help them? That's kind of how my groom got.

"If you'd learn how to use spices and make food taste good, it might be a different story."

And with that snide comment, the conversation was over.

This isn't to say that I wouldn't try again. It's not to say that I wouldn't just buy less meat when I did the grocery shopping. It's not to say that I wouldn't make different choices about my own personal diet that wouldn't affect other adults in my household.

It is simply an acknowledgment that living out a radical life of love, the kind that actually affects our day-to-day living, can be a potentially sticky beast for couples to navigate.

EXCUSES, EXCUSES

In case it wasn't evident, one of the obstacles that keeps me from living as radically and giving as generously as I'd like to is my husband.

Whoops! That didn't come out right.

It's probably more accurate to say that I often use my husband as an *excuse* to stay in the comfortable position that I really enjoy.

Yup, that feels better. This little maneuver, on my part, has proven true on any number of fronts.

In more recent years I've asked him, on at least one occasion, to get rid of our larger-than-life television. Seriously, this thing is so big it can be seen from a La-Z-Boy on the moon. I am convinced that I, and my children, would live fuller, healthier lives without it.

"If we didn't have this stupid thing," I say to myself, "I wouldn't even be sitting here, eating greasy popcorn and watching this mindless show."

I don't move my rear end, mind you, or turn the TV off, or unplug it or cover it with a beach towel. But because my husband acquired the dumb television at a laughably low cost from friends moving out of the country, it's sort of like he has a gun to my head and is forcing me to watch *Extra* for celebrity news.

PLAYING THE BLAME GAME

I let some time pass, realize how sinful I am and then nag him again. We usually play this goofy game every fifteen months or so. We do it whenever I've gotten a fanciful notion that involves him having to give up a habit, or eat less of something he likes or give more money to something else. It always ends with me getting the stink eye.

So I reason, *I should not push this. I should not jeopardize the peace of my marriage right now. I don't think that's godly. Even though I pretty much always do whatever I want to do the rest of the time, this is probably the moment for me to submit to my husband. Reverently.*

I hope you can see what's in that for me. If I suggest an unsavory game plan and he balks, then I get to feel as though I've boldly followed the leading of the Holy Spirit without ever really changing the way that I live.

Lest you think me insanely evil, however, none of this is premeditated. In fact, I've only noticed this disturbing pattern recently. And frankly, the dawning realization that God might be inviting me to change just *me* is a little bit of a bummer.

I'd so much rather take down my whole family with me.

In all sorts of instances I'd much *prefer* to blame my husband or my mom or whatever sinner at church baked the triple-fudge chocolate brownies for the ways that I fail to make faithful changes in my life. I'm a clever genius with this stuff. When, early in our marriage, my husband balked at hanging up the painting I'd made containing my proposed family mission statement, "Living Love Sacrificially," I felt that I was somehow not responsible any longer for doing it.

I am much more enthusiastic about monitoring and changing other people's behaviors than I am about noticing and changing my own. To be fair, it's kind of the human way. I believe that the recovery and mental-health communities have known this for a while. These wise folks will tell you that you can't change other people's behavior, but you can change your own. Which, of course, is not nearly as fun.

NOT THE WORST NEWS EVER

On my good days, though, I am able to recognize the inherent possibility in being responsible for my own behavior. When I'm thinking straight, I realize that I actually have the power to make little changes in my life that, over the long haul, can mean little changes for others.

In theory, for example, I could turn off the television and probably covet a lot less of the stuff I wouldn't even know existed if it weren't for all the television watching.

If I suddenly took responsibility for my own behavior, most likely no one would stop me from eating tasty goodies from the local farmers' market in lieu of a grain-fed Big Mac.

If I wanted to stop playing online solitaire to free up an extra hour every month or week or day to write to a child my family sponsors in India through Compassion International, I can't think of anyone who would stage any kind of protest about that.

I could probably even redirect my personal craft budget so that I'd have more to give to a local ministry. I don't think anyone would call the cops if I did that.

Sometimes it takes bold bravery to discuss, and disagree, and pray, and return to the conversation a week later to figure out with a spouse or with a close community what it looks like to be good stewards of shared time, talents and resources.

It *always* takes bold bravery to do it alone.

SARAH AND BEN

Another couple trying to navigate what it means to pour out their lives for others—when those lives have already been spoken for in marriage—are my friends Sarah and Ben. Both in their midsixties, Sarah and Ben have been married to one another for ten years. Ben is a salesman and Sarah is . . . a love fairy.

She really is.

Sarah used to be a social worker, matching children in need with adult female mentors through the national Big Brothers Big Sisters program. Now, without a paycheck, she's kind of a social worker for the world. Today she pours her life out, selflessly, for others. Whether she's caring for her aging parents or her grandchildren or one of the little sisters with whom she has stayed in touch, Sarah just drips with gracious, self-giving love.

She's kind of just joyful love with skin on. Ask anyone.

Recently I watched Sarah in action. Specifically, I watched how the hours of her day were gobbled up caring for others. Thinking of that very pull in my own marriage, I started to wonder how Ben felt about sharing Sarah with those in need.

When I asked Sarah about it, she confessed that the way she gives her time and talents and treasures to others *has* been a sticking point in her marriage, one that she and Ben have had to work through. "Ben knows that this is the way I am," Sarah explained. "I don't think he'd really want me to try to be someone different." Explaining that each of them brought different gifts and passions to the marriage, she affirmed, "We each have things that strengthen and change each other."

What that has looked like in Sarah's life is that, out of love for her husband, she has become more discerning about the ways she gives her time and talents and treasures.

Ben, though, has also been changed by his wife. With a gleam in her eye, Sarah brags about how generous Ben has always been, giving faithfully to his church and to various organizations. What's different now, she explains, is that instead of giving one thousand dollars to an organization, he's now willing to give it to an *individual* in need whom Sarah has roped into their lives.

It's still a work in progress. No doubt, it always will be. Wistfully, Sarah offers, "We work on it."

Figuring out how to be faithful to both a marriage and a world in need is holy work.

MARRIAGE ISN'T HALF AS BAD AS I'VE PAINTED IT TO BE

Did I just make marriage sound like a totally unsavory situation? My apologies both to the reader and to my awesome husband, Peter, who is such an authentic person that he allows our nuttiness to appear in print. There are actually lots of incredibly beautiful and creative ways that the kingdom is being built by married couples.

Penny and James attend my church. They're a white couple in their midfifties who do nothing to draw attention to themselves. They serve quietly, faithfully.

The first time I saw Penny and James at the Reality Center, I was terribly curious about what had brought them there. Each day after school, African American and Latino teenagers from the high school across the street flood into the Reality Center to play basketball, receive tutoring, enjoy free snacks, hang out with friends in the game room and participate in discussion groups. A lot of these teens come from broken homes. Most struggle financially. Some have had run-ins with the criminal justice system. A number have been expelled from school. Each needs love.

So when I stopped in at the Reality Center after school on an errand, I was a little surprised to see gentle James and patient Penny. In fact, my wheels were spinning in overdrive to figure out why they might have been there. Maybe Penny was doing some bookkeeping for the ministry. Or had brought a check by. Maybe James was dropping off some tasty snacks. Or fixing a rusty hinge. Any of those would have been entirely logical possibilities. What felt less likely was that James and Penny had come to hang out with urban teenagers.

When I finally got the scoop, however, I learned that that is exactly why they were there. Having just shown up and offered themselves as willing vessels a few months earlier, Penny and James had been assigned to play board games with any interested middle-school and high-school students.

Board games.

On any given day, this weird Brady Bunch scene would play out in the Reality Center's game room. By God's grace, some young person would walk right past the basketball court and pool table and Ping-Pong table and foosball table and sit down beside James and Penny. Together they'd play Scrabble or Monopoly or checkers.

What these young people experienced, of course, was so much more than learning how to play a few games they'd never played at home before. In the faithful, regular presence of James and Penny Fawcett, children who may have never experienced a healthy married couple were suddenly in the loving presence of a wife and husband who selflessly poured out their lives for the sake of the children God loves.

OFFERING MARRIEDNESS

Page and Ed are like this too. They're staff members of Navigators' Urban Hope ministry who live in my neighborhood. They share the lives of children by tutoring and coaching and loving. Peter and I took some squirrely neighbor kids to see their brother's basketball game on Thursday, and six-year-old Tee marched into the gymnasium and threw his arms around Coach Ed. In a community with more broken families than intact ones, Page and Ed offer kids their *marriedness*.

As a child who grew up in a home others would call "broken," I know a little bit what these young people experience in Penny and James and in Page and Ed. I know how bittersweet and *very* sweet it is to taste, even in a small way, what family is supposed to be. To this day, when I see a five-year-old girl, who has been waiting with her grinning mom at the airport, run into the open embrace of her father as he steps off an escalator and shout "Daddy!"—I breathe it in deeply, wipe away a tear and file the moment away in a box marked, "So *this* is how it's supposed to be."

Though it ain't always easy, married people who offer God their marriedness have a precious, irreplaceable gift to share with the new family God is building.

Now that you can begin to imagine what it might look like to build relationships with those *near* you

turn to page 175
MINDFULNESS
to discover how to
live in right relationship
with the beloved poor
who are less visible.

·· **21** ··

CAREGIVER

When a World in Need Poops on Your Pot

Whether you're caring for a child or an adult right now, whether the needs of this one are temporary or more permanent, you've landed at the right place.

MY **FRIEND SACHA IS THE MOST** kind and humble and compassionate person you could ever meet. There is not even one teeny-tiny mean bone in her body.

We were wrapping up our walk this morning when she asked what this book was about. Knowing how precious her kid-free, babysitter-on-the-clock moments are, I spit it out in fifteen short words: "It's about people with jobs and laundry and kids engaging with a world in need." When talking about what I'm doing I don't always throw in "kids," but I think that, since that's her life right now, I secretly hoped it would appeal.

That's when smoke puffed out her nose and fire came shooting out of her ears.

I really do think so highly of Sacha that my first thought was, *What-ever comes out of her mouth next—hopefully not vaporized lava—is going to be dead on.* She is such a thoughtful woman that whatever my lame synopsis had evoked in her was going to educate me.

"I'll tell you what I do not want to hear," she began. "I do not want to hear that my children should help me bake cookies to pass out to homeless people!" Did I mention that as a complement to her sharp thinking, she also has a beautiful, compassionate heart? Yes, I believe I did.

Then, for emphasis, she added, "The cookies would not even get baked!"

That's when I started to see where this was going. Sort of. I believe there is not a lot of extraneous baking happening in Sacha's home right now. She has three children, ages four and under, including a nursing infant. She spent yesterday in a doctor's office waiting room with aforementioned infant, waiting to get a full-arm cast put on the two-year-old. As you might guess, no one had had a good night of sleep. Though she happens to be married to a wonderful, useful guy, he travels for business and is away right now. So Sacha has got her hands full.

She railed on, "I don't want someone telling me to take my kids with me to the shelter while I serve dinner there, because my kids would not know if they were at a shelter or at a megamall. Don't *fool* yourselves! And I know moms have their kids bake cookies for soldiers in Iraq, but those kids can't even imagine what or where Iraq is!"

Developmentally, I do believe she's right. Perhaps sensing that she'd crossed a line, she dialed it back to entertain the possibility that possibly *somebody's* toddler actually did have a good grasp on the geography of the Middle East.

She admitted, "Maybe someone has a child who's prodigiously astute . . ."

She was on such a roll that she seriously said *prodigiously astute.*

Then, with desperation in her eyes, Sacha confessed, "I can barely get to the grocery store."

And there it is. If you're caring for someone with special needs, or just the regular ones, you're already pouring your life out for those who are weak and vulnerable. Your plate is full, and it may feel shame-heaping and guilt-inducing and crazy-making to focus on all the things you're *not* doing to bless the world God loves. The reality of your life is that you're most likely not in much of a position to add anything to what you've already got going.

Beloved friends who are caring for needy ones right now, be

gentle with yourselves and give yourselves grace. The world's poor are, at this moment, in your own home.

NEPAL, CLOSER TO HOME

Being overwhelmed by the responsibilities of caregiving isn't limited to baby-mamas and baby-daddies.

Yesterday when I saw my friend Gwen, she launched into our conversation with, "Did I tell you that I'm not going to Nepal?"

She hadn't.

I thought it was such a weird way to start a conversation that I kind of wanted to respond with, "Did I tell you I'm not winning an MTV Video Music Award?"

It would have been less weird had I known that she had been planning to go on a mission trip to Nepal with her church. Then the not-traveling plans would have made so much more sense.

I usually get pretty jazzed when affluent Americans are given the chance to see how the rest of the world lives. I've known firsthand the transformative possibilities inherent in these opportunities. So I immediately understood how not going to Nepal would be a loss for Gwen.

The reason she wouldn't be traveling, Gwen explained, is because her father-in-law, who lives locally, had recently broken his hip. Because her mother-in-law wasn't able to manage his care on her own, Gwen was needed to pitch in. So it's not even like she wasn't going on the mission trip because she'd won a free trip to Disneyland. She wasn't going because she'd won a free trip to "Take Care of More People Than I Do on Normal Days."

While it's not nearly as glamorous to care for an aging parent as it is to post a profile pic on Facebook of oneself holding a frail HIV-positive Nepalese baby, in a kingdom economy, these two aren't so very different.

In describing the types of folks we're invited to move toward, Jesus made particular reference to the sick and the naked and the hungry.

This listing, if I'm not mistaken, includes the ones recovering from surgery who can't yet bend over to tie their own shoes or hobble downstairs to the fridge for a bite to eat. By my reckoning, anyway.

If you're giving care to someone with a special physical or emotional or intellectual need, or if you're chipping in to care for a family member, or if you're staying planted where you are in order to be near a loved one stuck in prison, you're already ahead of the curve in this whole business about engaging with a world in need. In fact, you're a total rock star.

You should probably be writing this book.

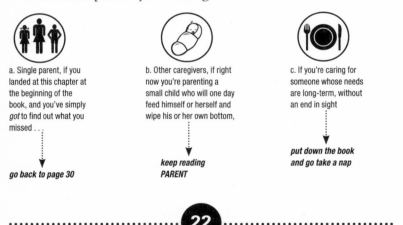

a. Single parent, if you landed at this chapter at the beginning of the book, and you've simply *got* to find out what you missed . . .

go back to page 30

b. Other caregivers, if right now you're parenting a small child who will one day feed himself or herself and wipe his or her own bottom,

keep reading
PARENT

c. If you're caring for someone whose needs are long-term, without an end in sight

put down the book
and go take a nap

●●●●●●●●●●●●●●●●●●●●●●●●●●● **22** ●●●●●●●●●●●●●●●●●●●●●●●●●●●●

PARENT

When a Little Child Leads, Get Out of the Way

LAST WEEK, SITTING IN FRONT of a bowl of bland rice and beans, the meal our family eats each week to remember the poor, my son demanded with not a little bit of irritation, "Why do we have to care about the poor?"

It often seems like children blurt out the things that grownups just *think*.

In a nanosecond, I realized that this might be the most important parenting moment of my entire career. Slowly, deliberately, I explained, "We care for the poor because God cares for the poor."

I was actually surprised to hear it come out of my mouth. It's not every day that I invoke God's name, either to defend my bad cooking *or* as a justification for whatever burdensome request I'm making of my children. If I'm going to drop the G-bomb in front of my kids—if I'm going to implicate God in whatever I've got cooking—I've got to be pretty sure that I'm not way off base.

I was *soooo* sure.

Because I'm pretty convinced that my job as a parent is to help my children encounter and grow in love for those in need, my children's feigned Monday-night misery only confirms that my husband and I are doing *something* right.

FINDING FAULT

In the award-winning movie *The Blind Side*, the affluent Tuohy family develops a heartwarming relationship with a homeless teenager in suburban Memphis. It begins when their son S. J. notices Michael at school, learns his name and begins a conversation with him.

My kids and I watched it together a few weeks ago on DVD. As the closing credits rolled, my eleven-year-old daughter scratched unpopped kernels off the floor. Reflecting on the plot, she concluded, "The whole thing was S. J.'s fault. Because he talked to him [Michael] at school and knew his name."

Though she might have chosen a word other than *fault*, my girl wasn't entirely wrong. The fact that young S. J. had already introduced himself to Michael at school did mean that the whole thing—the family's relationship with Michael Oher—sort of *was* S. J.'s fault.

But there's also this thing about a mother who is unwilling to drive by a teenager walking alone, at night, in the cold rain. There's the thing about a woman of privilege who is willing to push past all the normal human anxieties about differences and the unknown to open her home to a stranger. There's this very unlikely woman who calls that once-stranger *son*.

There's that.

In the end, there's just really no neat and easy way to pull apart a child's openness to welcome a stranger from his parent's willingness to do the same. Driving home from their private Christian school's Thanksgiving pageant, Leigh Anne Tuohy first learns Michael Oher's name by asking her son. But I suspect that her son *knew* it because of what he'd already learned from his mama.

TEACH YOUR CHILDREN WELL

Children take their cues about how to relate to others from their parents. When they watch us, they learn whether, upon encountering an Other, they should look away as if they'd seen no one at all or, with a warm smile, shake hands and exchange names.

Too often, however, as parents, we insulate ourselves and our families from the world's needs. Unchecked, we tend to operate this way. Propelled by a quiet—almost imperceptible—fearful whisper, we protect ourselves and our families from those who look and speak and sound different from us. We insulate ourselves from those who are uneducated or intellectually disabled or mentally ill. We protect ourselves from those who are sick and suffering. We keep ourselves from those who hurt or grieve. We might even avoid those whose Christian theology is decidedly different from our own! Unless we're pretty purposeful about moving beyond the invisible walls that separate us from difference and need and the unknown, we never fully engage with a pretty large cross section of the world God loves. Yet when we—dads and moms and neighbors and babysitters and uncles and aunts and friends—find ways around those barriers and over them and through them, our children finally have access to do the thing they do so well: love.

Most children aren't as naturally guarded and self-protective as many adults. I suspect this is one of the reasons why Jesus told us to be like them. If you watch how kids behave around pets and younger children—at least around the ones who aren't recently added siblings—they're often pretty compassionate to those who are weak, to those who are poor, to those who are sick and to those who suffer.

Our job as parents, as caregivers, is simply to give them *access*. That's it. That's the big plan. Because there's no shortage of suffering in the world, the only thing we really have to do is to not keep our children, and ourselves, from those in need.

A PAIR OF EQUALLY NEEDY NEIGHBORS

Andrea, who has a heart to love a world in need, is parenting three children under the age of five. If she's going to influence the world, which she longs to do, she's got to be a little creative about it.

Recently Andrea shared her frustration with me. "I was getting everyone into the car and our elderly neighbor waved to me," she explained. "I know she's lonely, but I just don't see how we're going to connect with her."

Little did Andrea know that she was preaching to the choir. Memories of my own little ones racing around my grandparents' retirement residence, one toddler-sprint away from fragile seniors being knocked to the ground, still haunt me.

"I so get that!" I answered. "How on earth do you take two little boys and an infant into this woman's living room, filled with breakables, and attempt to have a conversation? It's a mess, right?!"

"Exactly," Andrea agreed, sounding relieved that someone knew, a bit, what her life is like.

"Here's what I think you *might* do," I suggested. "Let the boys do their regular play, running around wild, in her yard where she can see them. On a rainy day let them draw her a picture and splash in puddles when they take it over to her. Take her out to Chick-fil-A and chat with your neighbor at the tables next to the play area." There are probably a zillion other things to try, but those are the first ones that came to mind.

Will Andrea be able to complete a satisfying conversation with her neighbor? Probably not. What she can do, however, by integrating her desire to reach out to love others with the stuff she's already doing, is to carve out a few of these opportunities that begin to connect her to a world in need.

Our job as parents is to not keep our children, and ourselves, from those in need.

Stuart also has two boys under the age of five. Stuart is in a hard parenting place where he simply cannot corral his rain-soaked children into anyone's foyer. Nor can he handle negotiating conflicts that come with the boy-wrestling which is guaranteed to ensue at Chick-fil-A. Although he can't possibly do much more than keep everyone alive during this difficult season, that savvy Stuart *was* willing to consider how he might begin to transform what he's already doing.

Specifically, he decided to tweak the way he does the library with his kids. For instance, he realized that, when one of them presents him with a stack of books to check out, it might be as simple as inquiring, "Did you want to find a book on recycling? What about earthquakes?" Without tacking on any extra responsibilities, he realized, he could invite his kids to explore the values near and dear to their father's heart. Implementing an entirely doable tweak, he exposes them to a world that's decidedly bigger than the one they'd know otherwise.

WHEN YOU'RE DECIDEDLY NOT FLUENT IN ARABIC

A few years ago my friend Erin was working from home, caring for a baby. Many desperate mothers, in this same position, have felt as though the only influence they have on the world is the diligent prevention of diaper rash. When that falls through, which it inevitably does, it can feel as though a stay-at-home parent isn't making even a fraction of the impact of Mother Teresa or Father Romero. Been there, felt that.

One day Erin was reading the worship bulletin from her church detailing the needs of the local World Relief agency. Noticing that another young mother needed a ride to the doctor, Erin figured, "If I strap my offspring into car seats, I can drive a car from point A to point B and back to point A. I can do that." A few days later, Erin took Amira, a recent refugee from Iraq, and her own toddler to the public health clinic. If you've ever experienced one of these places, you know this is no two-hour affair.

Early in the morning, approaching the desk at the public health clinic, Erin explained, "Amira doesn't speak English."

Looking up over a stack of paperwork, the desk attendant asked, "So you'll be translating for her?"

Without an Arabic word to her personal lexicon, Erin replied, "No."

Unfazed by the receptionist's look of disgust, Erin returned to wait with Amira. When Amira was finally seen, Erin listened to the doctor's assessment and later passed it on to Amira's grateful English-speaking husband, Ali.

What started as a simple taxi service slowly blossomed into a friendship. In gratitude for her ongoing kindness, Amira fed Erin wonderful home-cooked meals. Erin then spread the word about Amira's cooking and got her some customers for the home-cooked meals. Ali, quite the handyman, installed a new light fixture in Erin's home. Erin introduced Amira and her son to a nearby playground.

Without any particular plan about influencing a world in need, Erin's simple engagement with the least of these did exactly that.

I hope I didn't make that accidental situation sound too much like Mother Teresa–level heroics. It was anything but. The fact of the matter is that Erin was inconvenienced, naptimes at home in the crib were missed, and colds were shared.

I doubt Erin's tiny charges have yet been inspired toward service. What I *do* think, though, is that they have a mom who is more *whole* because she's bravely living into the vision that Jesus has for his followers. If you thought the best thing out there for parents is free childcare so you can sculpt a nice butt by taking five spin classes every week—well, that is not the good life at all. Rather, it's this thing about loving the ones who need to experience God's loving touch through human hands.

I also think that Andrea's kids and Stuart's kids and Erin's kids are learning about what it is to live life that really is life. Rather than being conditioned to believe that they deserve to watch hours on end of educational children's television programming, or deserve to be entertained at parks and craft stores, or deserve to be signed up for baby karate and toddler yoga, these kids are learning that, as a family that follows Jesus, they share life with those on the margins whom God loves.

Whether we as parents are shepherding a play date at the park or mulling over diaper choices or shopping for groceries or even choosing a story from a children's Bible, we can do it with a heart for the ones on the margins whom God loves.

COACH MUCKLE

As children get a little older, giving them access to the world God loves can, and will, look different.

Like so many soccer parents cheering from the sidelines, Dave and Kim closely tracked with the action on the field. Although they're not the kind to complain about how the coach treats their child, it did sound, to their ears, as if the coach were yelling at their son more than any of the other players. After the game, Dave checked in with his son.

"Why was the coach yelling at you so much?" he asked.

"Dad," Sam gently explained, "I'm the only kid who understands English."

Coach Muckle had started his team in 1999 by reaching out to kids who lived in urban neighborhoods of Pittsburgh. One of Coach Muckle's first players, an immigrant from Africa, had talked up the team in his ESL class at school, and word spread like wildfire. Soon the team had players from over twenty countries, including Peru, the Ukraine and Cote d'Ivoire. Convinced that technical excellence and tactical awareness could open the doors of opportunity to college and, in some cases, professional and Olympic careers, Coach Muckle drove his van all over the city to gather his team of players from their urban neighborhoods.

First of all, hooray for Coach Muckle, because he gets it. He had the vision to see that although all children are created equal, not all of them have access to equal opportunities. Hooray, Coach!

Second, hooray for Dave and Kim. Though their talented children would have had the opportunity to play on any number of local leagues, these parents—with a kingdom vision—chose for them to play with children they might not have had the opportunity to know otherwise.

See how *right* that is?

Whether or not we're able to squeeze one more car seat into our cars to accomplish humanitarian errands, Christian parents facilitate our children's experience of the world God loves as we chisel away doors and walls that would separate our children from it. When they're little, we teach them about the big world God loves. We let them join us as we embrace those on the margins. When they get a little older, we give them a little nudge and let them flap out of the nest and do it themselves.

OUT OF THE MOUTHS OF BABES

Sometimes parents lead like this. They allow, and even prayerfully orchestrate opportunities for, their children to encounter a world in need. Other times, it's the child who leads.

Dressed in their finest, Kylene and her seven-year-old daughter Chloe were jetting down the freeway on their way into the city to see the musical *Joseph and the Amazing Technicolor Dreamcoat*. On the way, they sped past a woman standing at the side of the road next to her disabled vehicle. Neither one spoke a word.

Silent echoes of the message Kylene had spoken so many times to her children as they'd driven past stranded *male* motorists intruded on their silence. "I will call the police to help that man," she would often explain, "but I'm not going to stop because it may not be safe." She'd kind of made a big point about the wisdom of not stopping for men and yet definitely stopping for women and children. I'm in complete agreement, because this is my own personal policy as well. The implication, of course, was that they *would* stop for someone less menacing. Yet they'd just hurtled by her at seventy miles per hour.

Kylene mentally crafted a cacophony of flimsy excuses. Yet each excuse fell flat as what many would call conscience continued to prick.

Before she was finished with her sophisticated rationalizations, Chloe beat Kylene to the punch. "You know how you've always said . . ."

"I know, I know. I'm turning around."

Sometimes parenting our children to embrace a world in need is as simple as paying attention and following their lead.

ONE WILLING FAMILY

This was true in the Salwen family. In a fancy schmancy house in Atlanta, the Salwen family was living the American Dream. Today, though, they're living another kind of dream.

Several years back, when fourteen-year-old Hannah and her father slowed to a stop at a red light, Hannah saw a homeless man on her right and a Mercedes on her left. Recognizing the blatant discrepancy, Hannah explains, "I looked at the guy in the Mercedes and said, 'You know, if that guy didn't have such a nice car, the man over here could have a meal.'"

That's the kind of naive way that children think, isn't it?

Hannah's father replied, "What if *we* didn't have such a nice car?"

Those were the opening lines in a family dialogue that led the Salwen family to engage in a pretty nutty experiment. In *The Power of Half*, Kevin and Hannah Salwen describe their family's decision to sell the fancy house and move into a smaller home that cost half as much. Having researched various charitable organizations, they took half the money from the sale of their home and invested it in initiatives to end hunger and poverty.

Hannah's younger brother explains, "We're showing that you can redefine the American Dream to mean that sharing can lead to a better life for others."

The Salwen family gets it. Taking their lead from a child—granted, one with a pretty alert and pliable parent—they were willing to recognize how much influence they really did have and courageous enough to use it.

SOME UNLIKELY BENEFACTORS

Nadia's family was sort of the opposite of fancy schmancy. In fact, while I was visiting a New Jersey congregation, I learned that Nadia, her seven siblings and their parents had just lost their home.

After sharing about Compassion International's ministry, I gestured to the back table where I had packets featuring children who were waiting for sponsors. Then I beelined to the back of the room to chat near the table. The first person to pick up a sponsorship packet was Nadia.

Nadia was clearly taken with the idea of sponsoring a child, and she started poring over the information with a friend. Because I don't like to let those unsponsored child packets get very far from my sight, however, I eyeballed her as she carried it around the room.

Honestly, I had some concerns. It may be because I'm a mom and I could see where this was headed. It just felt like one of those situations where a child brings home a stray pet that she's fallen in love with. (Note: I'm very clear that a child created in the image of God is not a stray pet. This was simply an analogy. Though you probably figured that out for yourself, I'll sleep better if I put it in black and white.) Then it's the mom's awful job to crush her heart and say, "No, that's not something we can take on right now." I simply did not have the imagination to see how this struggling family could add one more to their brood.

As I waited for this packet to land back on the table with a disappointed thump, and possibly some major attitude, I quietly noted others with whom I'd been talking who might *really* be able to sponsor that child.

Eventually Nadia's mother, who had been busy serving in the church kitchen, spoke to me about her daughter's harebrained plan. Expecting an apologetic refusal, I was quite surprised. This mother described, with delight on her face, how as a child she had sponsored a child with her family. She was absolutely thrilled for her children to have a similar experience.

She got it.

GRANOLA BOY

My friend Kristin's four-year-old son also has a pint-sized heart for the poor. Kristin and I were chatting last week when she told me about an incident that happened recently while she was driving around town with him. Apparently they'd passed a guy in the median, at a traffic light, who was holding a sign asking for help. After Kristin drove past him, her son insisted, from the backseat, that they circle back and give the guy a granola bar.

Kids say the darnedest things.

After sharing with me about her son's generosity, Kristin smiled and noted, "He has a good heart."

I don't really know. I've never met the child. Here's what I do know: Kristin's son has a mom who keeps a stash of granola bars in her car and is willing to go to the bother of turning the car around at the request of her four-year-old. This is one of those chicken and egg situations: which came first, the mindful mom or the mindful kid?

Though I can't say for sure, I'm certain that kids are blessed as parents make space for them to encounter and embrace those in need.

Parents are too.

 Parents, please keep reading on to explore a few of the nutty ideas about family you may be unaware of. I hope you're curious now.

23

FAMILY VALUES

Some of My Favorite American Idols

WE WEREN'T HOME WHEN THE LOUD sirens and horns of the fire trucks blazed down Buchanan Street. Driving home toward our neighborhood, though, we could see that traffic had been diverted around the 1000 block. As we pulled to a stop in front of our home, one of the kids on the street told us that there'd been a fire at twelve-year-old Rashawn's home.

When we arrived, the scene was still chaotic. Smoke smoldered from the burned-out side of the duplex Rashawn shared with many family members. It was clear that little, if anything, could be salvaged from the disaster. When Rashawn saw me, he came over to tell me that everyone was fine. No one had been hurt. Most likely, they guessed, a hot plate had caught fire. The family would be staying in a hotel, he assured me, and then the landlord would have another place for them to stay.

Firefighters who were finished with their work seemed to be waiting for whatever was supposed to happen next. In the dirt yard, some adults wept while others made calls on cell phones. Three toddlers waddled around the yard, being shooed away each time they tried to climb the familiar steps toward the front door.

It was the little ones who moved me. Actually, since the kids seemed unruffled by the crisis, it was the mamas and grandmas who'd have to keep caring for them who pulled at my heart. If there was one thing I'd learned as a mother, it was that children keep having needs. They keep filling their diapers. They keep getting thirsty and hungry. They need changes of clothes. I couldn't imagine how their caregivers could meet any of those needs in the midst of such a crisis. Wanting to give the family the dignity of some measure of privacy, we hugged Rashawn and returned to our house.

At home, I hopped in the car and headed for the grocery store. There I loaded up on diapers, wipes, sippy cups, crackers, apple juice and a gallon of water. On the way home, thinking about where I might buy a few outfits for the toddlers, I remembered several bins of children's clothing I had stored overhead in our laundry room when my own children outgrew them. These weren't just *any* clothes, though. These were the chosen fabrics into which I'd folded my most precious memories of my young children. We'd been given lots and lots of clothes when they were little, and once they'd outgrown them, I kept my absolute favorite little outfits folded safely away. One day, I dreamed, I'd pull them out for my grandchildren.

In that moment, though, the sentimentality with which I'd been perfectly comfortable for years suddenly struck me as borderline idolatrous. Though I could certainly afford to drive to a store and buy a few new things for the sooty toddlers, it seemed untenable to spend extra resources so that perfectly good clothing could go unworn for two more decades. It wasn't as if I had any illusions that my imaginary grandchildren would actually *need* any clothing. My hoarding wasn't about need at all. No, the purpose of the clear plastic bins with the tiny, neatly folded clothes was to ensure the warm and fuzzy feeling I'd have inside when I presented the treasures. Suddenly, keeping all the embroidered denim overalls, velvety purple ones, cute little T-shirts and tiny sandals cloistered away unused felt pretty hard to justify. When I got home, before I could change my mind, I shoved all the clothes that seemed most useful and androgynous into a garbage bag and threw it in my car beside the grocery store supplies.

After looping around a few blocks to park beside a traffic barrier, I dragged the heavy bags out of my vehicle and toward what remained of the family's home. After explaining to a firefighter that I wasn't the Red Cross, I asked Rashawn to point me toward one of the babies' moms. After quickly extending my little offering, I returned home.

Though I don't presume to think that my small offering could have eased a family's burden for more than a few hours, I harbor a hunch that it probably freed me from the heavy one I would have been toting around for decades.

BECAUSE I'M A BIG CHICKEN

As I was working on this book, I carefully avoided dealing with the ways we can be tempted to idolize our families. Because I'm a chicken.

Knowing I was writing about discipleship among those in need, though, a good friend innocently asked me, "Have you thought about talking about the evangelical view of family life and how we balance that with mission?"

I hadn't thought about that, but it sounded fascinating.

"I mean that sometimes we overly worship our family life and neglect the world," she continued. "It becomes an idol."

"Yeah, maybe you can write *that* book, and just let me say nice things about throwing granola bars through car windows at homeless people."

I balked, of course, because this is pretty touchy business. Asking questions about the choices people make in and for their families—especially around relationships and money and other resources—is really touchy business. This is offend-most-of-the-Christian-parents-I-know-and-love-in-one-fell-swoop business. So, I'm thinking I better just mention the ways that *I* have, at one time or another, been tempted to idolize *my* family.

Enjoy.

How I've idolized my family to the neglect of a world in need:

1. Preceding any assortment of family functions, I've spent too many dollars on special-occasion clothes to make my children look right in the eyes of others.

    Pretty good excuse: I'm honoring the occasion.

2. I've lived in affluent, homogenous neighborhoods that naturally separate me from those in need.

    Pretty good excuse: I'm honoring the other people in my household who don't mind the affluent homogenous neighborhoods one bit.

3. I've failed to invite strangers to share Thanksgiving and Christmas and Easter with my extended family because I don't want to upset anyone who has been coming for years and who is convinced that holidays are "family time."

Pretty good excuse: I'm honoring my guests.

4. I've let youth sports rule my Saturdays.

Pretty good excuse: It builds my child's self-esteem. Except when I'm screaming at them because we're late for the third game and they can't find their soccer cleats. And soccer balls. And socks. And uniforms.

5. I have spent hundreds—possibly thousands—of dollars photographing, videotaping and memorializing my family in frames and enlargements and albums and iron-on T-shirts and mugs and magnets and decorative quilts.

Pretty good excuse: As a creative soul, and especially as a visual artist, creative expression is how I'm made. So I'm kind of honoring the gifts that God has given me. With all the spending.

6. I've bought my children pricey backpacks, when their old ones worked perfectly well, simply because it was September and they were starting a new school.

Pretty good excuse: The new one will make them more confident when they go to school. (I mentioned I'm a genius at this, right?)

7. I've put my family first when I've meant to be committed to public schools that are in trouble—but accidentally got picked out of a lottery for a great public charter school and great public magnet school.

Pretty good excuse: Who am I to look a gift horse in the mouth? Shall I sacrifice my child's education for my loosely held ideals?

8. When I'm on vacation, I justify all sorts of nutty spending choices.

Pretty good excuse: This plastic souvenir will help my kids remember the trip. And the good time we had. Because we love them. And this trinket symbolizes, yea, *embodies*, that love.

9. I've allowed entertainment—like TV and DVDs and kiddie websites and video games—to supplant both shared quality time and any sense of family mission in the world.

Pretty good excuse: We all need the *down time*.

10. Oblivious to the world outside our doors, every member of my family has whined, on one lazy weekend day or another, "There's nothing to do-oo-oo-oo-oo-oo . . ." Of course there are things to do. In fact, what this actually means is, "We simply can't think of one more way to pleasure our small nuclear family of five people."

Pretty good excuse: Family time!

Basically, if you can think of an egregious insult to living a life of gospel love for others, I've done it. The problem is that, when my family's life is all about us, it is—de facto—not about others.

SERIOUSLY?!

I understand that most parents I know are not ready to label the cute clothes, the fresh backpacks and the smiley photo mugs *idolatrous*. On most days I'm not either. In fact, I'm very aware how difficult it is to entertain a whole new definition of heartwarming family life that does not include shared moments over sugary carbonated sodas, homogenous Thanksgiving gatherings and a photo album progression where Cub Scout uniforms are replaced by military ones.

The rub for Christians, though, is that this particular vision for the ideal family life was generated not by Jesus but by Norman Rockwell. An iconic painter and illustrator, Rockwell's sentimental paintings, which graced the covers of the *Saturday Evening Post* for half of the twentieth century, have gone further toward shaping American family life than any religion's authoritative texts. Tugging at our heartstrings, Rockwell's most popular paintings appeal to the anxious place inside each of us that longs for the soothing relief of safety, pleasure, certainty and comfort.[1]

One of the notable exceptions in Rockwell's collection, produced in conjunction with *Look* magazine's series on racism, is his 1964 depiction of young Ruby Bridges titled *The Problem We All Live With*. Marching bravely between four deputy U.S. marshals in front of a wall painted with racial insults, six-year-old Ruby Bridges, head held high, walks into her recently desegregated elementary school clutching a ruler, pencils and a few notebooks.

Now *that* is a Christian vision of family life.

Bridges' historic walk into William Frantz Elementary School in New Orleans reverberates with strains of the persecution predicted in Jesus' Beatitudes. It jives with his persistent mandate to lay down one's life. The starched, unstained dress of the despised, contrasting starkly with blood-red spatter from a tomato hurled in anger against a painted wall, evokes the bloodied image of a prior Innocent. This public moment in one family's life matches the cruciform pattern of discipleship into which Jesus calls his followers.

The Bridges clan was just a regular family, like yours. In fact, Ruby's father wasn't at all keen on her going to an all-white school, because he couldn't imagine blacks and whites ever being treated as equals. Her praying mother, though, was for it. She wanted Ruby to benefit from the educational opportunity that would give her more choices in life as an adult. Ruby's mother eventually convinced her husband that they had to move forward not just for Ruby but for *all* black children.

---

[1]When I recently enjoyed an exhibit from a national tour of Rockwell's collection, it was evident that his social consciousness, and depiction of a wider diversity of the American experience, found beautiful expression later in his career.

Rejecting the human predisposition toward safety and comfort, which was as popular in 1960 as it is today and will be a century from now, the Bridges family didn't choose for personal security. Instead, prayerfully, they chose for a different reality that had been painted first by Jesus: "Those who try to make their life secure will lose it, but those who lose their life will keep it" (Luke 17:33). Though the more popular *Saturday Evening Post* vision of American family life is all about making our lives secure, Jesus' vision for the women, children and men who are his followers is just the opposite.

As families, we choose every day whether we will live into one or live into the other.

DREAMS OF GRAND SMALLNESS

Right now I'm reading Scott Bessenecker's book *The New Friars: The Emerging Movement Serving the World's Poor.* In it, Bessenecker describes sending young adults off to live in solidarity among the poorest of the poor. These young people will live among those living in poverty who are forced to beg and prostitute in urban slums and garbage dump communities.

As these students and graduates respond to God's own invitation, some of them enjoy the support of their parents and families. Others, sadly, do not. As he commissions these particular servants, Bessenecker prays a special prayer for the ones whose families have not embraced a kingdom vision of downward mobility. His prayer comes from the heart of a father who would rejoice if one of his children one day embraced this special calling. This picture—of a parent who'd rather his child share the passions of their heavenly Father than live a life that's safe—really moved me. In fact, I got that pressure buildup right behind my eyes that happens right before a good cry.

Pointing an accusatory finger at Bessenecker, I extend my apologies right now to my husband and three children for the dreams and prayers I now hold in my heart for my babies. I simply did not know what to dream for until I saw it in print. It has always been my understanding that the American Dream is for children to grow up to be more financially prosperous than their parents. Now, thanks to Bessenecker, I'm convinced that these new dreams of grand smallness are so much better. I'm hopeful that as disciples of Jesus come to embrace the reality of the upside-down kingdom he ushered in, more and more privileged parents will begin to long for our children to have friends who survive off of other people's garbage.

God willing.

Now that you can begin to imagine what it might look like to build relationships with those near you, keep reading **MINDFULNESS** to discover how to live in right relationship with the beloved poor who are less visible.

·········· **24** ··························

MINDFULNESS

Yet One More Inconvenient Truth

THE POOR ARE ALWAYS WITH ME.

No, they really are.

The ones who live in my community are with me because Jesus has inconveniently opened my eyes to the guys who find shelter at the downtown McDonald's in bad weather. And good weather. The poor are with me because I can't ignore them when they sit at my table at the library and chatter noisily into their cell phones, even though it's a library and I went there to get away from noise in the first place. By the Holy Spirit, Jesus opens our eyes and ears to the visible (and audible!) poor who are all around us, calling us into relationships that require our time and energy.

The Spirit also alerts me to the presence of the *invisible* poor. Allow me to apologize, up front, for the rude designation. People who are invisible to many of us are, in fact, highly visible and keenly heard and intimately known by the Father who loves them and us. These are the ones in El Salvador who sewed the sweatshirt I'm wearing. They're the ones in China who packaged the almost microscopic iPod my daughter was given for Christmas. They're the ones in Bangladesh who can only dream of being offered gainful employment doing such sewing or packaging.

Over the last few years, I've become pretty convinced that I'm in real relationship with these invisible ones by virtue of the Father we share. Though we don't exchange birthday presents or grab a cup of coffee on Saturday mornings or take brisk walks together to increase our heart rates, our lives are inextricably bound. The presents I *do* buy and the coffee I serve houseguests and the shoes I wear for brisk walking are just a few of the ways our lives are bound together. Convinced that the way I use my resources— specifically the way I use my money—affects the lives of these invisible ones I cannot see, I've been on a journey toward mindfulness of the beloved Other.

Did that sound a little Buddhist? In fact, it has been *Jesus* who has convinced me that the way I steward my resources is not at all unrelated to the liberation of the poor ones around the globe whom he loves. What this means is that when I'm standing in the grocery store or the mall or the Stuffmart, I am *mindful* of the ones God loves whose hands laced the shoes I'm wearing. I'm aware of the ones who picked the coffee beans I'm buying. When I write a check or hand over my credit card, I attempt to be mindful of what type of business I'm supporting. Is it one that takes unfair advantage of their workers, or am I contributing to the liberation of the poor by purchasing fairly traded items?

One of my most pivotal moments on this journey toward mindfulness was the time I spent watching an online video called "The Story of Stuff."[1] This twenty-minute video educates consumers about the life cycle of all the stuff we consume, from the harvest of raw materials to the space our junk will eventually take up in a landfill. If you've not seen this video, or if it's been a few years, I implore you to watch it. Poke around the site to learn where your cosmetics, electronics and other favorite stuff has come from and where it's headed.

Though I wish it were not so, God's care for the poor, even and perhaps especially the ones I can't see, demands faithful stewardship of my resources. This intrusive awareness of my relatedness to the poor grips me in some of the most inconvenient places.

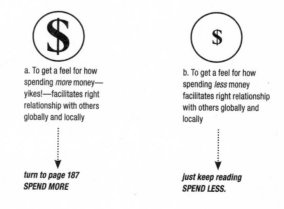

a. To get a feel for how spending *more* money—yikes!—facilitates right relationship with others globally and locally

b. To get a feel for how spending *less* money facilitates right relationship with others globally and locally

turn to page 187
SPEND MORE

just keep reading
SPEND LESS.

---

[1]You can find the video at www.storyofstuff.com.

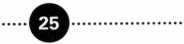

SPEND LESS

The Veritable Hazards of Cutie Foods

I **WAS AT THE GROCERY STORE,** minding my own business, looking for pie crusts in the frozen food section. Harmless, right? Before I found crusts, though, I accidentally stumbled upon the most darling little package of ice cream.

Apparently, you can now buy teeny 3.6-ounce containers of gourmet ice cream. Knowing that impulsive ice-cream buyers like to eat in our cars, they even come with a small plastic spoon right under the lid! Not unlike model airplanes or dollhouse furniture, the little package looks just like a miniature version of the classic pint-sized model. If memory serves, I paid about a dollar for each tiny, adorable serving. My kids loved them and probably ate a more reasonable portion of ice cream for an afterschool snack than they would have if I'd gone my regular route and bought a big, cheap generic half-gallon. That's what I told myself. I sort of framed it like it was about the health and well-being of my loved ones.

In order to do that, I kind of needed to not think about the wasted packaging that goes into these single-serving portions, let alone ones that come with disposable utensils. I also had to not think about locally grown produce that also might have fallen into the "health and well-being" category of afterschool snack options. And, as I was buying three one-dollar servings, I certainly couldn't think about children in developing countries whose family income was just two dollars a day—*if* a parent was fortunate enough to have work.

Once the thrill of the frozen find wore off, the reality of what I'd done began to sink in: with the resources which had been entrusted to me, I'd bought pricey, cute convenience food.

As horrified as I am purporting to be—as if I'd never done anything like this before—this actually happens all the time. In fact, spending money on what I don't need, consuming more food than I need and tossing away more packaging than I need is sort of a pattern. Regularly burning through way more than my fair share of resources, I've been unwilling to stop at *enough*.

WHEN LESS IS MORE

Enough can be a little unwieldy for North Americans like me to grasp. Because we're bombarded by advertisements insisting that we deserve more and more and more, *enough* can be a slippery concept for us.

In the book *Living More with Less*, which exhorts readers to live more justly and sustainably, a Canadian living in Calcutta shares how she discovered what *enough* meant.

Herta Janzen explains, "One day a mother came to our apartment to tell me that her daughter would be working in the mountains during the winter and needed a pair of warm slacks." (Because I'm aware that the word *need* can be as tricky to define as *enough*, I'm going to spell it out for you: slacks for a winter in the mountains qualifies.) Janzen continues on to describe how the mother asked her for a pair of hers. Janzen explains, "I had only two pairs—a bare minimum in Canada and the U.S. She would think that absurd. Were the Bible passages to be taken literally? After deciding which pair of slacks to give, I added the matching top as well. I'm embarrassed to admit now that I never missed that outfit. The remaining pair of slacks saw me through two winters."

I do not believe it's coincidental that Herta gleaned this little gem in Calcutta and not while pushing an obscenely stuffed shopping cart through the women's clothing section of an American megamart. Herta and her *two* pairs of slacks are light-years beyond most North Americans, because so many of us have trouble with *enough*.

Every once in a while, though, we manage it. I embrace *enough* when I decide, for a moment or a season, to not reach for gas station sodas or Gatorade or vitamin water or chocolate milks for $1.69 a piece because I have access to clean, drinkable tap water at home or even in the gross gas station restroom.

When a parent decides not to buy his kid a new backpack or soccer ball or wardrobe she doesn't need, even though advertisers try to convince him that, because it's back-to-school season, his daughter deserves them, he practices *enough*.

When I decide that the car I'm driving, while not the least bit cool, is entirely functional, I choose for *enough*.

When my husband bravely decides that our TV is adequate, even though it's a bulky tube television and not a flat screen, he settles for *enough*.

When a couple designing a new home can easily afford granite counters but chooses linoleum because it will serve their purposes, they decide for *enough*.

And when the same couple takes a long hard look at what they actually need and chooses to stay in the home they already have, they vote for *enough*.

As we live into the pattern of Jesus, trusting in God's good provision, we begin to say "No thanks" to that which we do not need. Though it's not nearly as much fun as saying "Just one won't hurt," or "I'll take one in every color," or "The largest flat screen you've got," or "Supersize me," it's a way that we walk—really walk—with Jesus.

We walk with Jesus when—on the spectrum between *too much*

and *not enough*—we do the radically countercultural thing of consuming what we need. Can you picture this zone that falls above *not enough* and below *too much*? Let's call it the e-zone. People fall into the e-zone when their daily needs are met. When they enjoy the food and shelter and clothing and medical care that their bodies need, they have enough. And when comfortable Christians like me choose to live in the e-zone—as opposed to the popular pleasure-myself-to-death zone—we make a little room for others to join us there.

JESUS AND ENOUGH-NESS

While *enough* wasn't literally one of Jesus' buzzwords during his ministry, the twin theological concept—the big idea about "daily bread"—permeates much of Jesus' message. In fact, *enough* is what helps me to understand one of the most confounding things that Jesus harped on. I'm talking about Jesus' somewhat tiring insistence that the ones who are lowly, poor and hungry right now are fixin' to move on up the ladder of prosperity, and the ones who are high, rich and fat right now might as well pack their Louis Vuitton bags and prepare to slide back down the chute of despair.

It's not just Jesus who is jazzed about this horrible situation.[1] Before she'd even been brainwashed by her son, Jesus' own mother, Mary, already knew that this surprising reversal was near and dear to the heart of God: "He [the Lord] has filled the hungry with good things, and sent the rich away empty" (Luke 1:53).

Psalmists knew about it. John the Baptist knew. Jesus' brother James knew. Others, like wealthy Zacchaeus and blind Bartimaeus, learned it firsthand.

Does this "reversal of fortune" theme sound at all familiar? Is it ringing a bell? All four Gospel writers heard Jesus saying pretty much the same thing: "Those who love their life lose it, and those

---

[1]By horrible, of course, I mean that I am rich, educated and comfortable. If I were poor, I'd think it was a fabulous idea.

who hate their life in this world will keep it for eternal life" (John 12:25). "All who exalt themselves will be humbled, and all who humble themselves will be exalted" (Matthew 23:12). "Whoever wants to be first must be last of all and servant of all" (Mark 9:35). "The greatest among you must become like the youngest, and the leader like one who serves" (Luke 22:26).

That's upside down, right? But what good does the radical inversion do if the oppressed poor are just going to become the rich ones who keep down the nouveau poor who used to be wealthy? Pointless, right?

Stay with me while I unpack the dizzying logic.

If the dramatic reversal of fortune only means that a different subset of people will be paying too much money to store all their stuff in crowded attics and basements and rented storage units, there's really no point. If it just means that new people will lack access to gainful employment, education and medical care, it's pretty much all a wash. It's just hard to imagine that's what Jesus, Mary and the gang had in mind.

But if the real blessing of the new kingdom means that everyone has *enough*, that's a completely different beast. What that looks like for the poor is that they, finally, breathe a deep sigh of relief that they no longer have to scramble after thin garbage scraps to feed their children because, at last, there is enough. What it looks like for the rich is that they, finally, breathe a deep sigh of relief that they no longer have to carry around the crushing weight of all the stuff that was supposed to make them so happy. At last, they can drop it and stop gathering more, because they have enough.

LISTENING TO QUIET VOICES

There are certainly lots of days I wonder if my *too much* even matters. Maybe it doesn't. Maybe I've just got too much free time and am taking this thing way too seriously. That's what I'd love to believe.

Living More with Less shares the observation of one missionary who lived in East Africa. Bertha Beachy notes, "North Americans find it very hard to believe that their wealthy ways of living affect poor people on other continents. But in Africa, people are fully convinced that North Americans and their actions strongly influence their lives."

I confess that I have to really concentrate in order to hear what my African sisters and brothers are saying. The voices of the poor simply aren't as loud or demanding as the ones constantly insisting that I deserve to satisfy my every whim. They're not taking out ads in Sunday's paper or buying airtime on Home & Garden Television. When I really focus, though, and when I do pay attention to the voices of the poor, I hear in them God's own wisdom.

Whether that reality—that my *more-than-enough* matters—becomes bad news for the poor or good news for them is up to me. And you.

What each one of us does with our *more-than-enough* is a decision that's already in our hands. It is bad news for the poor when my *more* is slowly dribbled away on sale-rack shoes and electronic gadgets and sewing supplies and rarely used tools that are just as easily borrowed.

It is good news for the poor, however, if, when I reach *enough*, I give thanks and do a little sharing. Those of us who have choices about what we do with our extra resources are invited into this wonderful possibility: that when we choose to spend less on ourselves, we have the privilege of spending more on what moves the heart of God.

Spend less. Love more.

LIVING IT OUT ON THE GROUND

Spending less demands that we develop habits that form a new pattern of consumption. And just so we're clear, spending less by scoring a cheap bargain isn't at all synonymous with faithful stewardship of resources. In fact, it's kind of the opposite. Rather, propelled by gratitude for *enough*, the new way—where we spend less—requires a good measure of creativity.

This can be achieved in one of three ways.

1. Petty theft and grand larceny

2. Deciding to do without whatever it is you want but don't really need

3. Sharing

By all means, begin with number two. Number one is ill-advised. Three can be way more fun than it sounds. If you're willing to consider it, read on.

1. Co-op

There is simply no good reason for every house on your block to have a ladder, lawn mower, leaf blower and chain saw. Spend an evening going door to door to inventory local resources among those willing to share. This really is as simple as Xeroxing and distributing your list. It's *that* easy.

For instance, on Friday night I was invited to a clothing swap. Everyone brought clothes they no longer wore very often, divvied them up by tops and bottoms and accessories and miscellaneous, then tried on ones they liked. The swap works best when it's gender-specific, what with all the disrobing.

Although most of the clothes were much too teeny for me, I really had fun. And scored a few great finds for my daughter. I learned about all kinds of new stuff. For instance, who even knew that "torso length" was a measurement? It is, apparently. One wise scavenger was even gleaning the smaller-sized clothes for the local, smaller-sized refugee neighbors in the community.

Can you see how this is *so* right? It makes for a lovely evening among friends. It keeps someone from buying retail when there are already so many clothes in the world that need good homes. It clears out overstuffed closets. It provides for people who actually need clothes, like refugee immigrants.

It's a win.

2. Borrow

In the absence of any organized system, just borrow stuff. Borrow it from the library. Borrow it from church. Borrow it from neighbors. Going camping with friends? Borrow tents, canteens, lanterns, pans, flashlights and mosquito netting. Going on a road trip? Borrow videos, a DVD player, books on tape, erasable whiteboards, winter weather gear, beach toys and sleeping bags. Going scuba diving on your honeymoon? I think you get the big idea.

Personal DVD collections are a great example of how we've been hoodwinked by advertisers. There's simply no good reason that most of us need to own ten or twenty or fifty DVDs. This became crystal clear recently when a friend, who had purchased a DVD for her daughter rather than renting it for one dollar through Redbox, told me, "You've got to watch it *twenty times* for it to be worth the money!" I could tell from my friend's tone that she realized the lunacy of the DVD math. I borrowed it from them—although I'm not sure I'd be able to sit through it twice.

I don't think Redbox is the answer. I think sharing is a win. I think renting from a locally owned and operated video rental store is a win. There are plenty of other options that do not involve people of affluence owning everything we can squeeze onto our shelves and into our closets.

Borrow, people, borrow.

3. Repurpose

Before you throw away old stuff, find a new use for it. Old curtains can be sewn into wonderful reusable holiday gift bags. Use printed T-shirts to make a cozy quilt. Decorate an old bicycle with twinkly lights to make a holiday sculpture. In lieu of a fancy backyard play structure, an old tire makes a great tree swing. These days the plastic containers my lunchmeat comes in are perfect for reuse; on any given school day, I can squeeze a sandwich, popcorn or pears into one.

Waste less. Repurpose more.

4. Freecycle

Freecycling is pure magic. Check online to find a Yahoo group near you.[2] Right now, a group of folks in your area are sharing car seats and yarn and videos and books and hangers and three-ring binders. Via an email listserv, members offer stuff they're no longer using and request stuff they need. Genius, right? It almost makes annoying hand-held technology that receives emails worth it.

Almost.

Within hours of posting a yellow twisty-tube slide, I got three takers. After searching six local thrift stores for soccer cleats, I posted my need on Freecycle and—voilà—cleats! Please consider becoming a member of a Freecycle community near you. It just makes sense.

5. Reuse

A lot of items that you might legitimately need—clothing to cover your naked body or chairs to allow you to sit during dinner—do not have to be purchased at your favorite retail outlet. Plenty of decent stuff in the world just needs to find the right home. Keep a running list of these items—plasticware, water bottles, raincoats, winter boots—and make quarterly runs to your local thrift stores.

If you've got kids, passing clothing along can be *really* easy. If there's a family at church that has children sized just a wee bit bigger than yours, put out the word that you'd gladly welcome a bag

---

[2]More on Freecycle at www.freecycle.org.

of used clothing. Then find the family with kids a wee bit smaller than yours and pass the bags to them.

6. Reimagine

Be willing to entertain the possibility that *it*—whatever *it* is—does not have to be done the way it has always been done. Quite often, no matter what *it* is, it shouldn't. Though few of us pause long enough to use any sort of ethical filter on some of the madness involving Halloween candy and birthday party favors and Easter egg hunts and Christmas stockings, it's probably time a few more of us did. To get you in the mood, please visit the Buy Nothing Christmas website.[3] I believe you'll be able to extrapolate the lesson and apply it to marshmallow ghosts and goodie bags.

Spend less. Love more.

*Now with all the money you saved buying less stuff, I'd like you to keep reading **SPEND MORE** to find out how to garner the stuff that you actually do need to buy in a store with integrity.

26

SPEND MORE

Not Nearly as Bananas as It First Seems

IN THE MIDDLE OF OCTOBER I got a notice in the mail, addressed to all registered voters, to bring a few extra documents to the

---

[3]Go to www.buynothingchristmas.org.

polls. Although I couldn't imagine what I'd need them for, I dutifully bent them and stuck them in my purse. Typically, I'm a dutiful sort.

Walking into an all-purpose room in the elementary school about four blocks from my home, I was happy to see that there wasn't a big crowd. I smiled and waved at my neighbor, Miss Harriet, a faithful volunteer at the polls. Flashing my driver's license, I signed off that I was who I said I was. Trading the identifying document for a ballot, I found an open booth and began making my choices.

When my ballot was complete, I walked over to the counting machine. I left a good distance between myself and the person doing business ahead of me to assure her I wasn't trying to peek at her ballot. When she took her "I voted" sticker and headed for the exit, I moved ahead for my turn.

"Pay stub, please," instructed the man attending the tabulation machine.

"Ummm, what's that for?" I asked, rifling through my messy purse. I hadn't read the entire notice I'd gotten in the mail; I'd just done what the simple instructions had told me to do. I assumed maybe they were doing some sort of nameless census survey to study income and voting. If they were, I wanted to do my citizenly duty by participating.

"Weighing the vote," the man answered, without much affect.

Unfamiliar with the term, I asked, "What's *weighing* the vote?"

"It's no big deal," he assured me. "I just type in your annual salary, or you can do it on the PIN pad if you'd prefer, and then your vote will be weighted accordingly."

"Sorry, I still don't understand," I answered, hoping for more information.

"It's just math. A ballot corresponding to a salary of twenty-five thousand dollars is calculated as twenty-five votes, and one with a salary of two hundred thousand is calculated as two hundred votes. It's not that complicated."

AM I BEING PUNKED?

I couldn't imagine that what I was hearing could be correct. I glanced quickly around the perimeter of the room, squinting for the hidden camera crew that was about to tell me I'd just been punked.

Fishing for more information, and aware that a line was forming behind me, I pressed, "And what about my neighbor who is out of work? How much is her vote worth?"

"This year," he explained patiently, "she's out of luck. But if things turn around for her next year, we'll be glad to see her."

"Are you *sure* this is how it works?" I asked, dubious.

"I'm sure," he assured me, glancing at the lengthening line. "Can we run yours now, or should I help the next person?"

"Next," I answered numbly, stepping aside.

I looked over at Miss Harriet to see if her face would give any indication whether or not I had eaten a bad burrito, slipped off to nap on the couch and woken up on Planet Crazy. Since these volunteers really aren't supposed to influence anyone, she didn't let on.

Still standing at the front of the line, my brain whirred in high drive as I tried to make a good decision. If I threw my hands up in the air and walked out, or taped my ballot to a timed explosive device and hid it in a nearby trash can and walked out, I wouldn't do anyone any good. But maybe if I voted responsibly, I told myself, I'd be able to do *some* good with my vote.

This is when I realized that the teeny pay stubs I'd brought along—for gigs I'd done over the year, articles I'd written and advances I'd received—didn't add up to very much at all.

"Um, Poll Guy?" I asked, raising my hand, as he handed the man ahead of me a little flag sticker. "Can I use my husband's pay stub?"

"Of course," he assured me, seeming relieved that I finally seemed to be comprehending and getting on board with the new system.

"I'll be right back!" I called to him as I opened the door and prepared to jog the four blocks to our home.

CRAZY TOWN

If U.S. elections were actually run this way, we'd be furious. Well, I suppose we might not hear a lot of grumbling from the ones bringing home six or seven figures, but most of us regular people would be pretty miffed. We wouldn't stand for it. Thank God that this is fiction.

Except it isn't, exactly. This is exactly how decisions about the distribution of the world's resources are decided: we *vote* with our dollars. Though we don't go into a privacy booth with a blue curtain, we dutifully cast our vote every time we spend at a cash register, purchase at a drive-through window or clickety-clack our credit-card digits into an online order form.

A paragraph describing one column on our checkout ballot reads, "To reduce the amount *I* have to pay for this good or service, I'm willing to buy products and take advantage of services whose costs have been borne by workers who don't receive adequate compensation or benefits for their labor." This is how I've voted when I've gone to Walmart to buy a T-shirt for five bucks. It's how I've voted when I've bought Levi's jeans at Ross for $3.99. Too often, I have knowingly scribbled a vote in the column labeled "Justice Negligent."

The other column on our checkout ballot reads, "I'm willing to pay a little more for the stuff I need to ensure that my dollars are being used to create a living wage for the ones I have to thank for the jeans on my butt." I've done this far less often, but I've done it when I've grudgingly peeked at a ranking of textile companies, evaluating their labor and social and environmental practices, before going shopping. Far less often, I have marked my ballot in the column labeled "Justice Pursuant."

Whether we like it or not, and whether it's fair or not, in this global economy the ones who spend the most dollars get to cast the most votes. Wherever we shop, the impact of these votes ripples daily around the globe.

So if you *have* them, where you put your dollars—or euros or rupees—matters.

In my own daily living, I am at times keenly aware of this. At other times, I am . . . uh, less so.

OXYMORONIC FASHION AND SWEATSHOP LABOR

I'd recently been complaining to my friend Constance that I didn't own anything that I could wear when speaking to a dressy crowd. For most of the work I do, I can get away with a T-shirt, jeans and Dr. Martens boots. For a few gigs a year, though, I would like to look professional.

After toying with buying a nice dress and high heels, I decided I couldn't pull it off. Whatever aesthetic gains I would achieve with the smoke and mirrors—I mean dress and heels—would be canceled out by forgetting to pack pantyhose and an industrial-strength razor for my legs. Or falling off the stage because I have no idea how to walk in heels.

Constance suggested I might try wearing a suit. The moment she said it I knew she was right. Now if *I'd* thought of it, I would have second-guessed myself. I would have worried that a suit was too mannish. But because the words had rolled off the tongue of such a stylish podium diva, I knew in an instant that my fashion troubles were behind me.

Time was tight, with just a few days before my next stylish gig. I decided that I was going to march right into Ross Dress for Less, quickly find a suit, try it on and buy it.

The first suit that caught my eye was a nice, tailored grey suit. I could tell at a glance that it was the right fit. I couldn't help but wonder, as I continued pushing back hanger after hanger, if this was going to be one of those wedding dress situations. Bridal lore has it that, after trying on three hundred poofy white dresses, you end up buying the first one you tried on.

What kept me from being satisfied with something that was good enough, however, was the same thing that drives so many compulsive shoppers. "What if they've got something in here, right now, that is more . . . *me*?!" And though I can't say I had a precise mental picture of which oxymoronic garment would scream both "professional" *and* "Margot," I was imagining something with a tailored waist in lime green or orange. For instance, if I had shoved aside a few plain black suits and come face to face with some sort of sherbet-colored garment with polka dots or broad funky stripes, I'd know in my heart that I'd found my suit. When that scenario did not transpire, I was forced to settle for grey.

"Look, look!" I begged my husband when he came home from work. "Won't I look like a big girl when I wear this?"

No sooner had I bragged to him about it than I got worried about the spending. We've been working together to tighten the old belt; new clothing, especially of the sort clearly destined to be worn rarely, might not be seen as a necessity. Because I knew that his pricey man-suits can cost a pretty penny, I added quickly, "Only $39.99!"

Having been trained by advertisers for decades to pillage local retailers with little thought for where my goods had come from, I suddenly realized that I had to start thinking about what I'd done. How on earth could my garment have been produced for forty dollars? How could an attractive lined pantsuit, with large pretty buttons, be made for so relatively little?

Suspecting he probably didn't care anyway, I quipped to my groom, "I don't even want to know how many people were exploited for me to get this suit for forty bucks."

With a mischievous twinkle in his eye, he replied in a soothing voice, "You're creating jobs. At least people working in sweatshops have *jobs*!"

With smoke pouring out my ears and laser beams shooting out of my eyes, I raged, "You are *kidding* me!"

Delighted to have set me off, he chuckled, "I'm joking. *Joking!*"

It's so hard to be sure.

BUYING ON THE CHEAP

I couldn't be sure not because he's a fiendish monster but because he's got a horse in the race. If I start caring about the people who grow my food and sew my garments and mold my plastics, the credit-card bill my beloved works dutifully to pay every month is not going to get smaller. It is going to get bigger. And there's the rub.

Integrity comes with a price tag that's bigger than the one stuck onto Convenience.

Thankfully, it's not always the case. Faithful stewardship of God's resources, loving others well with what we've been given: sometimes these things mean spending *less*. For any of us who make a habit of visiting our supermarket's holiday aisle—whether we're after neon plastic eggs or glow-in-the-dark wax teeth or a farting Santa doll—the road to better stewardship most certainly means spending *less*. (Turn to p. 180, SPEND LESS, for a fuller explanation.)

Loving others with the resources we use, though, will at times also mean spending *more*. Spending more on items that have been grown and manufactured and packaged by individuals who've earned a living wage for their labor—by buying Christmas presents at a Ten Thousand Villages store or choosing a fairly traded cup of coffee at Starbucks—is one way to honor those we can't always see.

Loving these often faceless Others, giving them the same consideration that we give ourselves—especially when we can pay the rent and feed our families and afford the occasional antibiotic—is a decidedly *Christian* value.

And though I'd love to proudly believe that somehow Christians have cornered the market on virtue, there's no evidence to suggest either that we're practicing this particular virtue or that people who aren't Christians are not doing it. There are plenty of other responsible, conscience-driven citizens of the world who care about justice and who *do* make these choices I'm describing. They spend more to buy chocolate that has been fairly traded. They pay a little extra for locally grown veggies. When they buy a book, they choose to do it at their local independent bookstore. They avoid using disposable plastic water bottles in order to reduce the amount of American trash being shipped for disposal in India. These ones have decided to act on a belief that the well-being of others is at least equal to their own well-being. Dissatisfied with prioritizing their personal convenience and pleasure above the needs of those whose faces they may never see, they make self-sacrificial choices about how they spend their resources.

And while non-Christians may be leading the charge on this one right now, it's worth noting that self-sacrifice, for the good of others, is pretty much the biggest Christian value we've got on the books. And though I see how it's a little dicey to compare paying extra for a very cool jacket from a socially conscious retailer like Patagonia to, let's say, the crucifixion of our Lord and Savior, they are not unrelated.

Stay with me as we flesh out this movement of giving ourselves to be *for* others.

You give yourself *for* others, possibly even sacrificing a teeny bit, by paying a premium price for what you wear that fairly compensates those who are responsible for the clothes on your back. For instance, I'm real clear that there's nothing valuable about owning a closet full of two-hundred-dollar sweatshirts. I will suggest, though, that—depending on the climate variance where you live—in lieu of purchasing a lot of cheap sweaters and impressive college sweatshirts and stylish coats to match a bunch of different outfits—owning one coat that's been ethically sourced is a choice worth considering.

Some good news is that what can offset the higher cost of buying equitably sourced goods is to buy *fewer* of them. See how everything just got easier? Instead of owning four or five or seven garments made on the cheap, in various colors and patterns, you might just own . . . one.

"One?" you might say. "Define *one* . . ."

It means what you think it does.

Though I'll confess I have been a little loose and free on the sweatshirt front—with various ones designated for sweating activities and outdoor, non-sweating activities and indoor, cuddly activities—I've come closer to hitting the mark on the heavy coat front. Before I moved from California to New Jersey, my mom bought me a fabulous wooly winter coat. This week I'll be pulling it out of winter storage for the eighteenth time.

Is it ratty? You bet. Does it still keep me warm? It really does.

BOTTOM LINE

Although it might feel like a big pain in the buttocks, this is worth attempting because justice for the poor matters to God.

When I read God's passionate pleas in the Old Testament for workers to be treated fairly, I simply can't *not* consider it. I'm compelled to listen and find meaning in those words for today. Oh sure, I'd like to believe that the ones Isaiah describes who were treating workers unfairly were billionaire CEOs who insisted that their employees work weekend overtime without receiving overtime pay, or that those CEOs went around ancient factories during their coffee breaks to slap the workers around a little. If that were the case, then I'd be off the hook (Isaiah 58:3).

When I'm honest, though, I suspect that today *I* am the one whose dollars and cents will affect the working conditions of the poor. Every time I cast my vote at the register, I declare what I believe in.

Spend more. Love more.

 a. If for some nutty reason you skipped over **SPEND LESS**, you have got to go back and find out why it makes so much sense as you purpose to love a world in need. Turn to p. 180.

 b. If you've read them both, keep reading to learn about the best-kept secret in a kingdom economy.

27

GIVE

Beyond Fat Wallets

A FEW YEARS BACK, A FRIEND and I decided that, because we had all we needed, for one year we would not purchase clothing. I'm happy to report that after a month or so of some major detox, it actually turned out to be pretty liberating. For the first time in years I could drive right past Target or T.J.Maxx without feeling desperately driven to stop in and find out what was inside. So the practice turned out to free up dollars *and* minutes.

What motivated the experiment in the first place was this whole thing about being in relationship with a world in need. Regretfully, what I did *not* do that year was purposefully redirect any of my fashion "savings." I would not have even known how to begin to do that math. If, previously, I'd ever been able to stick to a clothing budget, I would have been able to calculate what I might have spent and redirect the dollars. Since my standing modus operandi had instead been "when I see something I want, I buy it," the math was a little more complicated.

I doubt I'm alone on this one. Many of us, moved by Jesus' love for the poor, are practicing various disciplines of fiscal fidelity. We're eliminating sodas from our diets, or cutting out pricey lattes, or packing our lunches for work to reduce restaurant tabs. But if our principled living is not coupled with giving, we have simply fattened our own wallets.

"Brutal, Margot."

Right, right. The fat wallet comment is a little shortsighted, because there's more to it than the dollars. Two other things have happened too. When we embrace these disciplines we've also reduced the amount of plastic and paper refuse in the world, which is good for everyone. And we've been shaped by practicing mindfulness instead of pleasuring ourselves ad infinitum, which is also good. I guess I just want to be honest about how the poor—who certainly are the first to suffer the harmful environmental effects we inflict on the planet we share—do or do not actually benefit from the *savings* that were meant to honor them in the first place.

Ideally, eliminating waste from our spending frees up some of God's resources to be thoughtfully reallocated to those in need. Ideally. What we do with our savings—what we do with the excess once our needs have been met—is the real place where the rubber meets the road in a kingdom economy.

If you're anything like me, though, giving can get postponed to . . . never. Each time I opt against eating out, or refrain from buying sporting goods we can borrow, or skip dessert I don't need anyway—each time I do those things so that I can instead write a tiny check to local ministry that feeds the hungry, that ministry doesn't see one dime. Those calculations simply never happen.

I didn't want to spill those beans at the front end of the book, or even worry about any money beans at the get-go, because too many of us already choose check-writing over entering into any kind of relationship with the poor. But since we've touched on the stuff-buying, I'm compelled to make sure that giving is given a higher billing than "Ten Ways to Keep More Money in My Wallet."

PATTERNED GIVING

More effective than the mathematical minutiae of trying to give away $1.75 each time we forgo a twenty-ounce soda is being intentional about creating a rhythm of *patterned* giving in our lives. This means that we implement regular practices of giving that do not depend on tabulating a running total of the costs of the irresponsible impulse purchases we've recently resisted. I think you'll find the patterned giving to be so much more manageable.

Working on the assumption that you're familiar with the Christian practice of giving, I'm not going to spend much ink on the specifics. I'll bet you already know how it works.

Ministries that are doing great work, locally and abroad, will be more than happy to assist you. They can help you set up monthly giving, in which a designated amount can be automatically withdrawn from your checking account or billed to your credit card. Additionally, I'd love to suggest that—for your sake!—you couple one of these opportunities, either locally or internationally, with *relationship.*

1. Local Giving

One of the things I most love about the church where I worship is that a good hunk of the budget is allocated toward supporting a slew of missionaries and ministries. Another thing I love about it is that most folks in the congregation are actually *doing* ministry with their own bodies. In a myriad of ways, they're serving inside and outside the church's walls. It's a winning combo.

A few years ago, someone at church had the big idea of putting our bodies in the actual places where our local money is being sent. Rather than serving alone all over town, we'd choose two ministries, as a church, as the places we'd serve together. Cool, right?

If "your" monies, or your church's monies, are supporting local ministry efforts, that's the ideal place for you to begin to build relationships. Whether you tutor children or meet folks through a local shelter or pray regularly with and for an organization's executive director, let your financial giving be coupled with the giving of yourself in relationship.

2. Global Giving

You might naturally and logically assume that global ministry and relationship-building are oxymoronic. Though this is entirely understandable, it's not true in every instance.

The opportunity for relationship across boundaries of geography and race and language and culture and age and gender is one of the reasons why I am so wild about the child development work that Compassion International does. Compassion International has made the relationship between a child and his or her sponsor a priority in their ministry to children. As children's physical, social, educational and spiritual needs are being met through Compassion programs in their local church, sponsored children learn that their life matters to another, and matters to God, through regular communication with their sponsor. Through cards and letters and even online correspondence, a relationship develops as children write back, sharing both their lives and their prayers. It is truly a humbling and meaningful experience to share the lives of the children God loves.

Friends, this is God's work. The kingdom Jesus came to estab-

lish is being built as the lives of those who experience material
privilege and the lives of those who live with material want are
being knit together.

Get knit.

To peek at the ways that little
choices being made by folks just
like you are impacting a world in
need, keep reading **IMPACT**.

28

IMPACT

Bus Justice, Bake Sales and Big Dreams

THOUGH LOTS OF RELATIONSHIPS DON'T have a warm and fuzzy
Lifetime Movie ending, sometimes we get a glimpse into the kingdom impact that can happen when relationships are forged.

AVE MARIA

Maria is eleven years old. At 7:43 a.m., Maria's bus creaks to a stop at
the corner near her home. Climbing on, Maria plops down in the first
available seat. Three blocks later, the bus slows to a stop for a girl
named Nora. With an awkward gait, Nora reaches for a railing to
steady herself and climbs aboard. As she limps down the aisle, two
boys jostle her, and another shoots a spit wad that lands in her hair.
Another, talking to his friends, mocks Nora's slow speech. Nora slides
into a seat next to Maria. For both, it is a day like many others.

As Maria watches it all, she knows that she can't stay silent.

Later that day, on the way to the middle-school lunchroom, Maria quietly slips into the office of the school's vice principal. Nervous, awkward, she tells him what's been happening on the bus. She mentions a few names.

Beginning the next day, the boys lay off of Nora because one kingdom girl, propelled by love, is *for* her.

Sixth-grade girls have impact.

LEMON BARS AND CHOCOLATEY CHEX MIX

Every spring, Blacknall Memorial Presbyterian Church's fourth- and fifth-grade Sunday school class holds a bake sale. At 8:15 a.m., students start rolling in with chocolate-covered pretzels, blue cupcakes, lemon bars, peanut-butter buckeyes, chocolatey Chex mix and the occasional, exquisite apple pie. Blocking all entrances and exits to the building, the children hawk their wares. Shameless, they beg their own passing parents for quarters and dollars to subsidize their snacking.

This year the class raised $415.20. They voted to sponsor a teen going to summer camp with Reality Ministries, a local ministry that works with teenagers. Because of the generosity of these fourth graders, one teenage boy, living in foster care, was able to spend an amazing week discovering how precious he is to God and to others. Over the course of the trip, his inherent "lovability" was affirmed as he was loved radically.

I don't know exactly how these fourth graders decided to support Reality Ministries. I do know that several of them have older family members who have built relationships with teens there. This sort of thing can sometimes be contagious in families.

Ten-year-olds have impact.

AN UNLIKELY WORK UNIFORM

The life of a teen in rural El Salvador has also been impacted by fellow Christians. As a boy, Alejandro had no dreams for his life. The only road out of poverty that he could see was the gang life. When he was twelve, though, a woman at his church had a vision. In it, she saw Alejandro wearing a business suit and tie. Though I don't have stats on how many of these holy visions are eventually realized, I can say for sure that this one was pretty unlikely. Even Alejandro's own parents doubted.

"In our situation," they would say to him, "how would we see you in that?" You really can't fault them for being in touch with *reality*.

When Alejandro was matched with a sponsor, he began attending Compassion programs through his local church. There he heard a different message. Women and men in the congregation—with their faces, voices, bodies—confirmed that God had created him for a purpose. Alejandro learned, in his deepest places, that his life not only mattered to his parents but that it mattered to others in the body of Christ, to a sponsor, to God. As high school ended, his pastor encouraged him to apply for Compassion's Leadership Development Program. Based on Alejandro's grades, letters of recommendation and face-to-face interviews, he was accepted into the program, which provides university tuition and leadership training. The night he was accepted into the program, Alejandro remembered the woman's vision that had been prophesied over him at age twelve. With tears on his cheeks and a broad smile, eighteen-year-old Alejandro shares, "My family has changed their tune!"

Alejandro's response to being accepted into the program? He prayed, as never before, for his cousin—who'd been raised by a single mother—to receive the same scholarship. Upon finding out that his cousin Nixon had also been accepted into the program, Alejandro exclaimed, "What a great God!"

Today Alejandro is studying business administration, with aspirations to launch his own company of fresh juices.

A pastor and members of a local church congregation, equipped by Compassion, poured their lives into Alejandro. In God's mercy, a sponsor paying thirty-eight dollars per month enabled Alejandro to participate at the Compassion program in his local church. By that same mercy, a praying woman impacted Alejandro's life. Each one had impact.

ALEJANDRO'S IMPACT
But Alejandro's own impact may just outshine them all.

Alejandro leads a drama troupe that creates and executes performances to communicate to others the hope they have in Jesus Christ. I witnessed one incredibly powerful performance that illustrated some of the hard choices faced by children raised in poverty. This group of Christian teenagers is influencing lives each time they perform in their church and community.

When I visited in May, Alejandro, his cousin Nixon and their friend Miguel, also in Compassion's Leadership Development Program, were planning a special motivational event for the children in their community. Until these three young men were chosen to attend university, the only "successful" role models local children had were gang members. Alejandro, Nixon and Miguel now have a strong desire for these children to see all that is possible if they apply themselves and do well in school. As leaders in their community, they are casting that vision for children.

One of the guys who traveled to El Salvador with me in May, a young musician named Chris Zobac, was deeply moved by Alejandro. Chris is a founding member of the band Two Cent Offering. Seven months after returning home, Chris explained, "Alejandro made a major impact on me. I am so thankful that I was able to meet him and hear his story. Ever since our trip to El Salvador, I have been praying for him and we've also been in contact through Facebook."

When Chris learned that Alejandro was in need of a new sponsor, a much greater financial commitment now that he's at the university level, Chris explained, "I've prayed to see him reach his full potential and have the opportunities that the Leadership Development Program brings. I've prayed that his sponsor would write him letters and encourage him. God has answered those prayers by allowing *me* to sponsor Alejandro."

A lot of folks would think that Alejandro was lucky to meet Chris. I suspect, however, that Chris—and the rest of us who got to know Alejandro—would say that Chris is the one who is blessed.

I only bring up Maria and the fourth graders and Alejandro to make a point: kingdom relationships are changing the world. If these pretty unlikely redeemers have an impact that changes lives—which they clearly do—then you do too.

 If you're convinced that kingdom friendships are the way that Jesus' kingdom is being established—which I hope you are—keep reading **INFLUENCE** to learn how to invite others into the fun.

INFLUENCE

Roping Others into Kingdom Shenanigans

RON JAY IS A GRAD STUDENT. He's married and has two little kids. On the side, he's building relationships with teenagers through Reality Ministries, in Durham, North Carolina. At Reality, volunteers develop friendships with teenagers, many of whom come from difficult circumstances.

Ron Jay is particularly close to one teen who, like Ron Jay, is a gifted musician. When Ben's life was recently turned topsy-turvy, Ron Jay shared this email with the community that loves them both.

> This morning, Ben's home was broken into. They came through the window and took as much as they could carry, including their electronics and all of his musical instruments. The cops said that they might try and come back for the rest, so everyone is obviously on edge. Please pray for this lovely family as they navigate the emotions of losing both their possessions and their comfort and safety. I had hoped to get some of Ben's close friends in on a little graduation gift for the spring, but this event may hasten the getting and giving. Let me know if you'd like to help. Thanks for being there for this family right now.

Ben's friend Ron Jay couldn't fix the wrong that had caused his friend to suffer. What he could do was to incarnate the near, loving, steadfast presence of the One who loves Ben and his family. He could spend time listening to Ben and the rest of his family.

He could also invite others in their community to love Ben's family. He could invite others to pray for them. He could invite others to pitch in for a new guitar. He could put out the word that they were looking for a lawyer, willing to work pro bono, who'd help them get out of their lease.

Ron Jay gave himself, and used his influence, for the sake of a friend.

LEAH'S LETTER

A few years ago I received another holy email from my friend Leah. If you're technology-averse, and are convinced that nothing good can come from the Internet, I'd beg you to reconsider your position. At the very least, tweak it.

Leah's email to me could have been an invitation to a cooking-equipment party at her home, where she'd get credit for every sale. It might have been a request to connect on LinkedIn. It might have been a series of funny pet pictures with humorous and inspiring slogans.

It wasn't.

Leah wrote:

Dear friends,

Merry Christmas! I am writing to ask you to participate with me in something wonderful this Christmas season. For the past several years I have sponsored two precious girls—Teresa in Bolivia and Janelle in the Philippines—through Compassion International, an organization that seeks to release children from poverty in Jesus' name. Compassion works in partnership with local churches to educate, disciple and care for children in twenty-five developing countries. My family has sponsored kids through Compassion for many years, and we have always been impressed with the organization's integrity and commitment to meeting the kids' physical, educational and spiritual needs. One of the best things about sponsoring kids through Compassion is that it is relational: in addition to providing monthly financial support for their education and care, I exchange letters and photos with my girls to encourage them and remind them that I love and pray for them. For me, this is the best part!

Unfortunately, the number of kids waiting for sponsors has exploded in the past year. I am looking for a sponsor for a beautiful six-year-old Colombian boy named Juan who is in kindergarten and loves playing soccer. He has a family that loves him, but the educational and spiritual support that he receives from Compassion is essential to helping him develop to his full potential. I hope that you will consider becoming a sponsor!

Love, Leah

Leah used her valuable social capital—which is what made me click open the email in the first place—on behalf of the vulnerable ones God loves. Her influence, along with the other nineteen ways the Spirit had gently nudged me that month, was what moved me to sponsor my first child through Compassion.

A FATHER'S HEART

Joe is a guy in rural northern New Jersey who works for a company that makes those plastic air-filled things that get packed in shipping boxes to keep stuff from breaking. Joe is married to Tracy, and ever since they dated thirty years ago, Joe and Tracy wanted to have a big family. Four years after marrying, they had their first child. When Kaitlyn was six, the couple realized that they would be unable to have more biological children.

When they decided to adopt, Joe and Tracy expected to receive a Caucasian baby, but the child the agency chose for them was East Indian. After three years together, the family received a call about a little girl who was available for adoption. She was also a child of color. Three years later, they received their fourth child. At that point, they thought they were done. Then they received a call saying that another little girl needed a home. They said yes. Just over a year later, the phone rang again, saying that another little girl needed a home. Today the couple's six beautiful children, ages two to twenty-three, include those who are Caucasian, African American, Indian and multiracial. You'd think six kids would be enough. You'd think that becoming family to five children in need of homes would be enough. You'd think. But it's not enough for Joe and Tracy.

Joe and his wife haven't put in their paperwork for another child. Rather, they recognize that their purpose now is to encourage other families to consider adopting the children who are waiting for forever families, especially those who are waiting in foster care in New Jersey. Right now Joe is busy putting together a gala evening of education, inspiration and tasty treats for families considering responding to God's leading in this way. Both Joe and Tracy are passionate about children, especially the ones waiting for families. It's clear that God's unlikely plan for precious children in the New Jersey foster-care system is a regular Joe and his wife in rural New Jersey.

Joe and Tracy had eyes to see that, in a world in need, the holy relationships God had ordained for them to embrace were as close as a phone call away. Today they're helping other people catch the vision and are influencing children's lives forever in the process.

YOU ARE THE PLAN

A kingdom vision of relationships that cross social, geographic and cultural boundaries is spread as Jesus-followers rope others into God's holy shenanigans. More often than not, this happens when disciples connect with others at points of passion. It happened when Ron Jay the musician started sharing life with a talented young performer. The vision spread when Leah, who has a doctorate in health policy, seized an opportunity to facilitate relationships in which children's physical, social, educational and spiritual needs would be met. Joe, a devoted father, is inspiring other families to welcome waiting children into their families.

Frederick Buechner says it most eloquently: "The place God calls you to is the place where your deep gladness and the world's deep hunger meet." Graciously, God knits together relationships where the well-fed and the hungry are nourished by one another. As you cross barriers to build relationships that celebrate your passion, invite others to do it with you.

Are you a kid person? When you partner with a local church or one in a nearby city by joining a mentoring program, invite a colleague from work to join you.

Are you a foodie? Gather three friends and serve a meal—a really tasty meal—at a local shelter. Plan to make a new friend there who loves tasty flavors as much as you do.

Do you build? Grab buddies and spend a Saturday morning working on a Habitat for Humanity house. Then take Habitat's prospective homeowner out for coffee afterward and really get to know him or her.

Are you passionate about the plight of the lonely? Call your local office of The Arc to learn how to volunteer with Special Olympics. Then invite your friends and neighbors to cheer on your new buddy.

Holy friendship with the stranger can be a little bit contagious. Become a carrier.

If you've read this book straight through from the introduction, you've now been exposed to 314 not-so-hard ways you could be influencing the world as you allow Jesus *in* you to move *through* you toward the ones he already loves.

Because that is, admittedly, a lot to keep track of, read on to learn six principles you can apply to your particular circumstances that will help you as you take a single step toward a world in need. (Since six and one are so much more manageable than 314.)

TRANSFORMATION

Implementing Some Holy Tweaking

BELIEVE I SUGGESTED, toward the beginning of this volume, that to build relationships with the folks God loves whom you don't yet know, you don't need to *add* a bunch of stuff to your life. Breathe easy. It's still true.

While you don't need to add lots of extra activity, you should plan to invest a little energy into thinking about how to transform the stuff you're already doing. My hope is that this process has already begun for you.

Your journey with Jesus into a world in need won't look exactly like your friend's journey or your mentor's journey or Shane Claiborne's journey. The adventure into which Jesus is calling you— one that utilizes the unique gifts and passions and concerns and experiences and resources that have been assigned to you—is entirely unique. As you navigate what shape this will take, it's worth keeping a few guidelines in mind.

1. Do it *simply*.

Don't think that this week you've got to start eating vegan, sponsor three children overseas, adopt a child from your state's foster-care system, write a big fat check to Blood:Water Mission and invite a homeless friend to stay in your spare room.

Give yourself at least *two* weeks.

Just kidding. Seriously, the way to start is with just one thing. I feel pretty confident speaking for the Almighty when I say that God is not expecting you to single-handedly save the world. As we move with Jesus, our job is simply to ask, "What's the *next* thing you have for me?"

For instance, if today you cannot participate in a demonstration for humane wages and working conditions for farmworkers, you can educate yourself and decide not to eat at a convenient restaurant being boycotted for using suppliers that don't treat their workers fairly—even though your niece is badgering you to go there for the Barbie Yummy Meal toy. If today you can't solve the problem of the United States' addiction to oil, you might still be able to walk or wheel to the nearest store to buy the gallon of milk you need. If today you cannot find the wherewithal to lobby Congress to participate in providing affordable childcare to working parents, you can probably offer a night of childcare to those overwhelmed parents so that they can have a date night.[1]

The only person in human history who can single-handedly change the world for the better has already done it. Today you're being invited to live into that invisible reality, just one step at a time.

Don't freak out, people. You can do this. Do it one step at a time.

2. Do it *creatively*.

Right now, just release any dreadful notions of what it means to engage with a world in need. Let go of whatever paralyzing ideas and images you have that involve potentially awkward social situations and imaginary shifty poor people taking advantage of you. What Jesus had in mind is so much better than *that* dreadful scenario.

Last night I learned that the board of Reality Ministries recently voted to incorporate under their ministry umbrella (New Horizons

---

[1]Though some of these structural changes might not feel manageable for you today, they're still necessary. To learn more about what you can do, check out Adam Taylor's *Mobilizing Hope: Faith-Inspired Activism for a Post–Civil Rights Generation* (Downers Grove, Ill.: InterVarsity Press, 2010).

School of Academic Excellence) a high school for teens who haven't succeeded in public schools. Eating my potluck mac and cheese, listening to the update, I had the funniest first-row-seat view of Jesus' upside-down kingdom.

Each time a staff person described the circumstances that have brought these teenagers to New Horizons—whether they have been defiant with authority, expelled from public school, involved with gangs or engaged in criminal behavior—their faces seemed to light up a little more, shining a little brighter. Even the board members who had just voted to embrace Jesus' leading in taking on this pricey new commitment glowed a little as the off-putting descriptors were listed. Watching these faces shine at the opportunity to know and minister among those who have been written off by the world but whom Jesus so deeply loves—it was a winsome little kingdom moment.

Since no one is throwing big money at either these unlikely students or the small staff that loves and mentors and teaches them, some of the teaching will be done by volunteers. And right here is where it gets even more creative and wonderful. Reality Ministries has recognized that there are a number of stay-at-home parents in our community, mostly moms, who have a bunch of extraneous diplomas lying around their houses. Earnestly believing that these adults would be blessed to participate in what God is about at New Horizons, Reality Ministries is offering these parents childcare for the hour a day they'd be teaching in the classroom. I hope you can see how good this is for students and how good it is for stay-at-home moms and dads. If their young kids are usually home alone, then learning how to share toys, play games they didn't choose and respect a new caregiver is good for the kids too.

This kind of creativity—meeting the needs of others to free them up to join God's work—is simply brilliant. As you think about how to engage with a world in need, feel free to get wildly creative about how you do it too.

3. Do it *courageously.*

I recall my surprise when, after moving to California to attend college and trolling around in my friend's convertible one day looking for a parking spot at the beach, my friend prayed for the Lord to provide a good parking space. Young, malleable, I simply assumed that my friend, with faith to move SUVs, was more spiritual than I. I also made a quick mental note to start asking God for *way* more stuff than I already was. Though thrilled when the spot magically appeared as if by wizardry, I continued to harbor a nagging little wondering about the kind of God who would place such a premium on my convenience as to orchestrate a pleasing outcome to that prayer. Though this odd religion of comfort and convenience has effectively saturated the United States of America, it's simply nowhere to be found in the Gospels.

Choosing inconvenience takes courage. To have suggested to my friend while we were back at campus that, as Christian stewards, we ride our bikes to the beach—or wait fifteen whole minutes for the next bus—would have taken more guts than I had. Despite what we've been told about a God who has nothing better to do than to make our lives easy, discipleship is inconvenient.

When I could purchase my family's groceries, son's soccer cleats, daughter's school supplies and a toy for my niece's birthday under one big-box roof that I suspect is profiting off underpaid workers at home and abroad, it takes a huge effort to *not* do it. Frankly, I don't always succeed. Remembering to buy locally grown produce on Saturday mornings, finding a kid from church who has outgrown his soccer cleats, researching which local retailer is the most socially responsible provider of school supplies and walking to the local Ten Thousand Villages store to pick up a gift for my niece is a *ton* of work. Though a little bit of planning can probably make it more manageable, I find that making good choices is usually terribly inconvenient.

It takes real courage to follow Jesus into uncomfortable situations—which is so often where that holy rascal seems to lead. It takes courage to share one's resources boldly. It takes courage to ignore the opinions of others. It takes courage to consume less. It takes courage to displease one's own children in the effort to teach them simplicity. It takes courage to speak truth when it's easier to remain silent. It takes courage to give one's affluent relative a simple card on Christmas morning that explains that a goat has been donated to a needy family in her name.

If you're serious about loving like Jesus loved, you *will* be inconvenienced. You will be less comfortable than you are now. You might even get flak from people you love and respect.

I believe that Jesus might have mentioned that this stuff would probably happen. When it does, you'll just know you're on the right track.

4. Do it in *community*.

My friend Susan regularly draws me into whatever kingdom shenanigans she's got up her sleeve at the moment. Yesterday's email began, "Wonderful Margot, I am working on an idea and I wonder if you might possibly like to be involved in my wild hair scheme . . ." It's never a bad idea to start these requests with flattery.

Because her scheme had nothing to do with unmanageable hair at all, I believe she combined *wild-eyed* and *harebrained*. Neither was entirely off-base. This week's schemes are "Come give a presentation to the potentially disinterested teens to whom I voluntarily teach public speaking at New Horizons Academy" and "Let's spring our friends' baby out of pricey daycare by creating a web of folks to care for him since his hardworking parents really can't afford the daycare right now."

I don't think Susan could have known that I've already prayed for God to send more teachers to New Horizons. I know I never mentioned to her that the family of Baby Cuddlebug had been weighing heavily on my heart but that I hadn't been able to see any possible solution to their pickle. Possibly the Almighty clued her in.

I put up with all of Susan's monkey business and even agree to it because when I do, I get the amazing privilege of being a part of what God is doing in ways I wouldn't have come up with on my own. Susan never needs to be apologetic about asking yet again, because I am the one who is, repeatedly, blessed.

Discipleship is a team sport. You're made to follow Jesus with others. If you want to join a tutoring program happening at an inner-city church, be like Susan and drag a friend along with you. Or plan to make some new ones there. If you want to coach Special Olympics basketball, take one of your old high-school teammates. If you want to volunteer at a local psychiatric hospital, invite a teen from your church to join you. Moving toward those on the margins isn't something you're expected to do alone.

5. Do it with *integrity*.

By integrity, I don't mean upstanding moral character, although that's fine too. Rather, look at the structure of your life and *integrate* fresh practices of hospitality, compassion, kindness and generosity into what you're already doing. Engaging with a world in need isn't about removing you from the life you're already living. Instead, it's about integrating compassion into the rhythm of the life you've already got, patterning it to conform to the life of Jesus.

A variety of small practices can reshape you from the outside in as you begin to let your eating and shopping and texting be informed, and transformed, by the person of Jesus and by your relationships with the ones he loves. Practicing sabbath—resting from your work or cell phone or Facebook—makes you available, in fresh ways, to God and to others. Fasting or forgoing meat or modifying your diet in some other way to honor the poor will make you more alert to their suffering. Joining your community for prayer, either daily or weekly, will begin to shape your heart and actions.

Choosing one day of the week to do your shopping, once you get used to it, liberates you for other things. A consistent faithfulness to these small practices sets you free to be *for* others.

6. Do it with *anticipation*.

Jesus is not asking you to throw away your life and your longings. Quite the opposite, in fact. As you choose to move toward the weak, you can expect to meet God. Henri Nouwen explains, "Jesus' life is marked by an always deeper choice of what is small, humble, poor, rejected, and despised. The poor are the preferred dwelling place of God. Thus they have become the way to meet God."

You can expect to meet Jesus as you embrace this adventure of moving into deeper relationship with a world in need. It's not just that Jesus is *sitting* among the poorest of the poor—though I have every reason to believe he is. You also experience his nearness as you move in the ways and directions he's moving. Like the disciples on the road to Emmaus, whose eyes were opened to recognize Jesus in the breaking of the bread, you can expect to experience Jesus' nearness as you walk with him, chat with him, eat with him and move with him toward the world he loves.

Right now, take a moment to locate where you find yourself in relation to Jesus. See him gently curling his pointer finger, drawing you to himself, to move together toward a world in need. Then—without either lollygagging or rushing ahead—take one step with him.

You're at the end of the book. Lay down the Kindle or shelve the paperback in order to lift your eyes and move your feet toward the world God loves. Which was sort of the whole point of the book in the first place.

Start again with a group of friends. You'll find an appendix of Bible study and discussion questions at the back. ·····························➤

RESOURCES

• Baby Steps

AWARENESS

Take our online quiz to find out how well you're loving your neighbors on the margins. You can find the quiz on the Facebook page for *Small Things with Great Love*.

Enter your annual household income to discover how you rate: **www.globalrichlist.com**

Find out how the products you use every day are made: **www.storyofstuff.com**

EDUCATION AND INSPIRATION

Join the conversation about how Christians are living lives patterned after Jesus: **www.redletterchristians.org**

Be nurtured and challenged as you seek to follow Jesus: **www.conspiremagazine.com**

Learn how socially and environmentally responsible your favorite brands and retailers are: **www.betterworldshopper.org**

• Next Steps

ACTION

Find the stuff you need—for free!—and find good homes for the stuff you don't need: **www.freecycle.org**

Purpose to do Christmas differently this year: **www.buynothingchristmas.org**

Engage with other Christians committed to practicing love and justice in the world: **www.sojo.net**

GIVING

Partner with Compassion International to release children from poverty in Jesus' name as a monthly sponsor: **www.compassion.com**

• Big Steps

SHARE YOUR LIFE

Locate an intentional Christian community near you to connect and learn more: **www.communityofcommunities.info**

Spend a year as a missionary in an urban neighborhood: **www.missionyear.org**

Serve in the inner city for a summer or for a longer internship: **www.urbanpromiseusa.org**

THE ADVENTURE
CHALLENGE

UNLIKE A LOT OF BOOKS, whose authors hope that you "can't put it down," I actually hope you will.

Ideally, as your Christian imagination is ignited by small things, you'll set this book down and respond to the Spirit's tug by taking one small step. It is kind of cool that you are the only person in the world who can connect the dots between Jesus' heart for a world in need and the neighbors whose lives touch yours. This study guide is meant to help you do that. Specifically, it can help you identify the particular ways in which the ideas discussed in each chapter can be fleshed out in your situation.

Spend some time with these questions, being expectant that the Spirit is inspiring, leading and equipping you. Jot down ideas as they come. Write the names of neighbors who come to mind or descriptions of the ones whose names you'd like to learn. Notice the kinds of opportunities that energize you. Share with a friend how God is leading you.

Then . . . put this book down!

Oh sure, you can finish reading it. You can even discuss it with your small group or Sunday school class. I hope you do. But then set it on the coffee table and go take that first small step with great love.

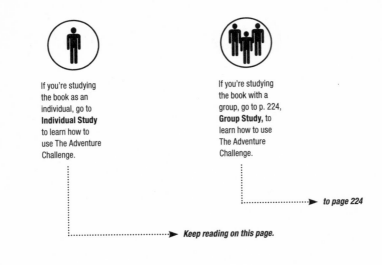

If you're studying the book as an individual, go to **Individual Study** to learn how to use The Adventure Challenge.

If you're studying the book with a group, go to p. 224, **Group Study,** to learn how to use The Adventure Challenge.

to page 224

Keep reading on this page.

Individual Study

Note: Before you begin working through the study guide questions, go online to take our short quiz to find out how you rate as someone who engages with a world in need: www.margotstarbuck.com/smallthingsquiz.

USE AN OLD NOTEBOOK OR JOURNAL with some fresh pages left as you move through this study guide. Because you can *expect God to meet you*, you're going to want to have a written record of your prayerful musings. Your insights and questions and noticings and wonderings open you up to God's leading. A record of what God is doing in your heart right now will prove to be a treasure as you grow spiritually.

You can expect to meet God here.

For your journal work:

1. Pray

God of love, Father of Jesus, here I am. Open my eyes to see your face and open my ears to hear your voice. Speak, Lord, your servant is listening.

2. Reflect

a. What struck you or stuck with you from the last study?

b. Describe how you did or did not respond to the adventure challenge that you chose last week. What meaning do you glean from how you did or did not respond?

3. Questions

Work through the study guide questions provided. Be sure to keep your responses intimately tied to your particular life circumstances.

4. Adventure Challenge

Choose just *one* of the adventure challenges from this week's study and jot down how you hope to respond to it during this next week.

5. Pray

God of mercy, Father of Jesus, fill me with your love for the world. Guide me as I move toward your beloved ones. Grant me courage to love in your name.

One tip: keep your study focused on *your* role in bearing God's love to a world in need. This isn't a theoretical academic inquiry! It's all about paying attention to those particular places where God is leading *you*.

Group Study

Note: Before your group begins to study Small Things, *encourage participants to take a short quiz to find out how they rate as someone who engages with a world in need. You can find the quiz at www.MargotStarbuck.com.*

Discussing the quiz is a great icebreaker at your first meeting!

Do you know what a springboard is? It's that bouncy thing that gymnasts jump on before flying through the air toward some unwieldy apparatus. These questions are meant to be a springboard for your discussion of *Small Things*. Not all of the sections for each week will apply to each person. Group members should engage with the sections that are most relevant to their circumstances. The discussion can then—ideally!—be tailor-made to fit your particular group. We mention this to give you the freedom to let your conversation wander off where it may.

At the beginning of each group:

1. Prayer

Open with prayer, asking the Spirit to guide the group's conversation.

2. Reflect

Ask the group: What's one thing that struck you from last week's conversation? Was anything particularly surprising or convicting or challenging?

3. Challenge Check-In

Ask the group:

a. Which adventure challenge did you choose last week, and how did you respond?

b. Is there meaning to be gleaned for you in the way that you did or did not embrace the challenge?

During each group:

4. Discussion Questions

Move through the questions provided. The six-week study guide will help keep your group moving in the right direction.

5. Ending the Discussion

Stop the discussion ten minutes before the group is scheduled to end, to leave time for a leisurely wrap-up (see below). If it's helpful, designate the most anxious person in the room—or the one itchiest to get out on time—to be the timekeeper.

At the end of each group:

6. Think Back

Invite people to share one thing that they'll take from this week's conversation.

7. Adventure Challenge

Invite each person to share which adventure challenge they've chosen and how they hope to engage with it.

8. Prayer

Invite one member to close in prayer, asking both for God's guidance and for the courage to respond in love to a world in need.

One tip: Keep your study focused on *your* role in bearing God's love to a world in need. This isn't a theoretical academic inquiry! It's all about paying attention to those particular places where God is leading *you*.

A Six-Week Study Guide

WEEK I: CHAPTERS 1-5
The Big Idea and How We're Wired

1. **THE PLAN**

   Read Matthew 25:31-46. Knowing what your daily life is like, begin to imagine (journal or discuss) what each of these might mean in your context:

   a. food for the hungry

   b. drink for the thirsty

   c. hospitality for the stranger

   d. clothing for the naked

   e. care for the sick

   f. visits to the prisoner

   Don't be afraid to get creative! (For example: taking sippy cups to a local shelter, or serving lemonade to the crew doing landscaping at your church.)

   ADVENTURE CHALLENGE: Choose one of these invitations above that makes sense for you to embrace this week.

2. **BIBLE**

   Read James 2. Which verse feels most surprising or radical or challenging? What would it look like to live it out?

   ADVENTURE CHALLENGE: Is there a "poor person" (James 2:1-8) in your life right now who you can shower with dignity, loving him or her the way you love yourself? Describe how you'll engage with this beloved one.

3. **AWARENESS**

   Read Luke 16:19-31. Where have you chosen to squeeze your

eyes shut to the world's need? Describe the opportunities, if any, you've had to see poverty up close and personal. How did these experiences affect you?

ADVENTURE CHALLENGE: *Make one small choice this week to stay aware of the world's needs. (Be specific; otherwise, you might not do it!)*

4. OUR OWN

Read Deuteronomy 15:7-8, noticing how God expects the Israelites to care for their "own." Other verses mandate the Israelites to care for the orphan, the widow and the alien. Which are the first faces that jump to mind when you think of those who are your own? Outside of this intimate circle, do you have a sense that there are *particular* people God has invited you to call your own? For example, it may be that you have a special heart for orphan care, or racial reconciliation, or nursing homes. Where do you sense God leading you today?

ADVENTURE CHALLENGE: *Prayerfully ask God to open your eyes to one person you might begin to love as your very own. Pray for this person daily.*

5. STRANGER

Jesus' encounter with a Samaritan woman in John 4:1-42 crosses boundaries of gender, race and religion. With whom do you find it hardest to connect: someone across lines of age, gender, race, language, class, education, income, religion, politics, ability or sexual orientation? What type of person, right now, feels most like a "stranger" to you? Where might you connect with someone like this?

ADVENTURE CHALLENGE: *Take one practical step this week to move toward a beloved child of God who is demographically different from you. (Share who this is with the group to give the challenge some real traction.)*

Remember, just choose *one* of these adventure challenges to embrace this week!

WEEK II: CHAPTERS 6-12
Noticing How We've Been Made

Answer questions for either chapter six or chapter seven.

6. EXTROVERTS

Look at the ministry opportunities happening in your own faith community and identify the ones most naturally suited to extroverts. If you're an extrovert, where has your extroversion been used for the kingdom good? Did any new possibilities in this chapter trigger your imagination?

ADVENTURE CHALLENGE: Extend yourself in friendship to one person—someone you cross paths with in your regular routine—who might be lonely. (What is his or her name?)

7. INTROVERTS

Look at the ministry opportunities happening in your own faith community, and identify the ones most naturally suited to introverts. If you're an introvert, where has your introversion been used for the kingdom good? Did any new possibilities in this chapter trigger your imagination?

ADVENTURE CHALLENGE: Of the six opportunities listed at the end of chapter seven, embrace one this week. Or create a fresh one!

Answer questions for either chapter eight or chapter nine.

8. MEN

Read Mark 10:35-45 and identify how you do or do not find yourself in this story. Name those areas of life in which you are most driven to be recognized as significant or important. King suggests that you convert the natural impulse toward greatness to become first in love, first in generosity.

What has or what could that look like in your particular situation?

ADVENTURE CHALLENGE: *In one small way, step into upside-down kingdom greatness this week by choosing for smallness. What, exactly, will this look like for you in the next seven days?*

9. WOMEN

Read Matthew 5:14-16 and consider the impact you have in the world. Do you consider yourself a tiny candle flicker or a high-wattage spotlight? List some of the ways that you have real influence—in the way you use your time, energy and resources—both inside the home and outside the home. Did any of these surprise you? Also, name the places to which you have, by virtue of your gender, easier access than men. Unpack the kingdom possibilities.

ADVENTURE CHALLENGE: *Go online and print off contact info for a local women's shelter. Post it in a public women's restroom in your church, school, grocery store or place of employment.*

Answer questions for one of the following chapters (ten or eleven or twelve).

10. YOUNG

Read 1 Timothy 4:12. Do you perceive that others look down on you because of your age? As you think about engaging with a world in need, what about your current circumstance lends itself to flexibility and possibility? What about your life today feels as though it keeps you from the poor? Prayerfully offer both of these back to God.

ADVENTURE CHALLENGE: *This week create a journal entry, saved as a file on your computer, that describes your hopes, dreams and commitments for engaging a world in* *need over the next decade. Ask a like-minded friend to do the same. Share these with one another, commit to pray for each other and check in regularly.*

11. MIDDLE

Create a thorough list of the social networks to which you've belonged, past and present: clubs, organizations, teams, denominations, congregations, alma maters, employers, online networks, etc. How are you using these, now, for the good of others? Where do you see potential?

ADVENTURE CHALLENGE: Do you know someone who's out of work? (If not, your church secretary can give you a name.) Choose one:

a. *Post "I have a friend who'd be great at _____ and needs a job!" as your Facebook status and see if you get any bites.*

b. *Scroll through www.craigslist.com to see if you can find anything that looks like a good fit for this friend. (This can be super-fun treasure hunting!)*

c. *Create your own plan to connect someone in need with the resources to which you have access.*

(Which one of these has your name on it this week?)

12. OLD

Read Psalm 92:12-15. Do you know anyone like Susan who, in retirement, has looked beyond her or his personal family circle and been "fruitful"? What is he or she up to? Name the places where your energies are being spent on those who are different from you. Where have *God's own* become *your own*? Where do you see possibilities?

ADVENTURE CHALLENGE: Dream about what your life could be during this season by brainstorming a list of kingdom possibilities. Share this with someone you trust.

Remember, just choose *one* of these adventure challenges to embrace this week!

WEEK III: CHAPTERS 13-18
Accounting for Our Current Locations
Answer questions for chapter thirteen or fourteen or fifteen.

13. SCHOOL

Read John 13:34. What "others" do you think Jesus means? From chapter 13, what is the first rule for loving a world in need? Who are the folks on your campus who are most easily overlooked? (How many of them can you greet by name?) What are the opportunities on your campus, both local and global, that allow you to engage with a world in need?

ADVENTURE CHALLENGE: In the next week, learn the name and story of one individual who works on your campus in one of the lowest paying jobs—e.g., grounds, food service or custodial.

14. WORK

Read Colossians 3:23-24. What does this mean for you? Is there a way in which your particular job intersects with a world in need? How? If there's not an overt connection, can you think of some ways that your work does, even tangentially, affect the experience of the poor?

ADVENTURE CHALLENGE: Identify one small step that you can take in your workplace this week to either (a) connect personally with someone who is less affluent or (b) affect a system in your workplace that could positively change the experience of the poor.

15. HOME

Read Hebrews 13:1-3. What are the ways that you are, or might be, moving outside your home to engage with a world in need? What are the ways you are, or might be, inviting folks who are demographically different from yourself into your home? Describe the obstacles you anticipate or experience.

ADVENTURE CHALLENGE: Learn the name of one person in your weekly routine who you do not yet know—e.g., someone at the grocery store, cleaners or pharmacy. Describe which person, in your natural orbit, you plan to meet this week.

Answer questions for chapter sixteen or seventeen or eighteen.

16. URBAN

If you live or work or worship or play or shop in an urban environment, in which particular places is the world's need unavoidable? Where do you brush up against it? How have you responded?

ADVENTURE CHALLENGE: Visit a house of worship where folks in your community who might be marginalized by race or income worship.

17. RURAL

Identify the people at the center of your natural social circle. Now: who are the other folks that are living on the far margins of your rural community? Where are the places that your lives do, or could, overlap?

ADVENTURE CHALLENGE: Visit a house of worship where folks in your community who might be marginalized by race or income worship.

18. SUBURBAN

Name the places where folks who are poor do move through your community, either to work, to receive services, to worship or for some other reason. Where are the points at which you have connected with those who are poor?

ADVENTURE CHALLENGE: *Visit a house of worship where folks in your community who might be marginalized by race or income worship.*

Remember, just choose *one* of these adventure challenges to embrace this week!

WEEK IV: CHAPTERS 19-23
Considering Our Family Situations

If you're single and caregiving, hop down to chapters twenty-one through twenty-three.

Married? Or single and kid-free? Answer questions for either chapter nineteen or chapter twenty.

19. SINGLE

Name some single heroes—both the historic ones and also the ones you know today—who have been builders of God's kingdom on earth as it is in heaven. Is there a particular gift that your singleness allows you to share with others? Read Isaiah 43:1. To what degree do you feel embraced and cherished by God? Has the body of Christ reflected that reality in your life?

ADVENTURE CHALLENGE: *Consider and take one small kingdom step this week that could not be as easily achieved by someone married or parenting. (Be creative!)*

20. MARRIED

Read Hebrews 10:24. Is there a way in which you and your spouse spur one another on to love and good deeds? How has engaging with a world in need looked in your marriage thus far? Are you the spouse who is more reluctant to move toward a world in need, or are you the one more eager to embrace relationship with those in need? Identify the challenge that God might be putting before you right now.

ADVENTURE CHALLENGE: Take responsibility for your own movement toward a world in need this week by taking one small step of which your spouse is not aware!

When others are in your care:

a. If you care for *particularly* needy ones, answer questions for chapter twenty-one.

b. If you're parenting those who are more self-sufficient, answer questions for chapter twenty-two.

c. If you'd like to compare a popular view of family life with a Jesus-view of family life, answer questions for chapter twenty-three.

21. CAREGIVER

On a scale from one to ten, how do you feel you and your charges are doing at engaging a world in need? (*One* means that you're trapped in your dwelling, working on toilet-teaching while someone who runs around all day without undies is peeing on the floor. *Ten* means that your five-year-old has launched a nonprofit that provides clean drinking water to war orphans overseas.) Describe how satisfied and/or frustrated you are with your self-ranking.

ADVENTURE CHALLENGE: Do nothing. For this day, your "small thing with great love" is giving yourself the gift of grace. (And maybe praying for under-resourced caregivers in situations around the globe.)

22. PARENT

Read Proverbs 3:1-4. Are there ways in which you've attempted to turn your children's hearts toward God's commands to care for the poor? What is it that moves the heart of your child? (Animals? Babies? Sick kids?) Are there ways in which you've nurtured that compassion? Are there ways in which you've shared your own passion for a world in need with your child?

ADVENTURE CHALLENGE: *Take one small step to allow your child to engage with a world in need. Find one way to cross barriers of comfort and security this week, for the sake of nurturing your child's heart.*

23. FAMILY VALUES

Identify some of the ways that you may have placed family, instead of Jesus and his values, at the center of your priorities.

ADVENTURE CHALLENGE: *This week, take a small step that helps your family break free from self-centeredness. Embrace a challenge that is uniquely suited to your family. Will you shut down pixilated screens to break an addiction to entertainment? Will you use "family time" to engage with others? Will you redirect one meal's dining-out budget to those who are hungry?*

Remember, just choose *one* of these adventure challenges to embrace this week!

WEEK V: CHAPTERS 24-27
Living Mindfully of Beloved Others

24. MINDFULNESS

Read Proverbs 28:27. Would you say that the eyes of your heart are open or closed to the poor? Chances are that you affect the experience of the poor with most of the purchases you make! Describe how meaningful, or decidedly not meaningful, this reality is to you. Does it influence your decisions? Will your choices change at all?

ADVENTURE CHALLENGE: *Go online and watch the Story of Stuff. Then, for starters, notice on food and clothing labels what country your resources originated in. Pray for the people whose hands have provided your stuff.*

25. SPEND LESS

Read Matthew 6:11. We express gratitude for our daily bread when we stop at *enough*. Describe your relationship with enough-ness when it comes to food, clothing, technology and other "stuff." (If you collect a certain kind of item, for example, will your collection ever have *enough*?)

ADVENTURE CHALLENGE: This week, target your food consumption as a place to practice* enough. *Embrace the spiritual discipline of stopping at* enough *by eating what your body needs and not what it wants. (This really is a radical experiment for most Americans.) If you struggle with disordered eating, or if you have in the past, skip this challenge or apply it to a nonfood area of your life, such as the money you spend on other shopping habits.

26. SPEND MORE

Read Proverbs 14:31. Do you see any ways in which your spending choices contribute to the oppression of the poor? How does this idea about loving others by spending more money—to obtain equitably sourced goods—sit with you? Is there a way you're doing this now? Where might you begin? What feels like the biggest obstacle?

ADVENTURE CHALLENGE: Identify one item that you typically consume and that is produced locally; purchase it this week. (Potential markets include farmers' markets, grocery stores that stock locally grown produce, neighbors or colleagues who sell eggs from backyard chickens, etc.)

27. GIVE

Read Matthew 6:1-4 (NIV). Notice whether Jesus says "*if* you give to the needy" or "*when* you give to the needy." Describe what your giving habits look like right now. Does any of your financial giving correspond to relationships you're developing? How might you begin to develop a relationship that follows the path in which your giving monies flow?

ADVENTURE CHALLENGE: *Write a letter to someone who benefits from your financial giving. This might be a sponsored child, an overseas missionary that is sponsored by your church or the director of a local agency in town.*

Remember, just choose *one* of these adventure challenges to embrace this week!

WEEK VI: CHAPTERS 28-31
Embracing the Possibilities

28. IMPACT

In John 8:1-11, after Jesus graciously delivers a woman caught in adultery, the next words we hear from him are, "I am the light of the world" (John 8:12). What does Jesus say in Matthew 5:14? Can you identify ways that you are being light in the world God loves, especially in relation to the poor? In this chapter, we looked at some pretty unlikely heroes who have influenced the lives of others. How convinced are you that *your* life can influence others like this?

ADVENTURE CHALLENGES:

a. Local: Minister to lives close to home. Whether you work with youth or have a heart for one of your neighbors or have noticed someone at church who seems lonely, take one *step toward someone this week with great love.*

b. Global: Prayerfully consider whether sponsoring a child —or sponsoring an additional child—might have your name on it. Visit www.compassion.com to learn more.

29. INFLUENCE

Read Acts 2:42-47. How is the influence of God's people in

the world *corporate?* Your impact in the kingdom that Jesus is building multiplies as you invite others to join you. When has someone roped you into loving a world in need? When have you invited someone else to join you? Share the outcomes.

ADVENTURE CHALLENGE: This week—in person or by phone, text or email—invite one other person to join you in moving toward a world in need. (Ideas: Invite a teenager to join you in the church nursery. Grab a friend and create a special surprise gift basket for a mutual friend who is stressed. Ask a colleague to bake cookies with you to take to a local shelter. Possibilities are endless.)

30. Transformation

Your journey toward a world in need is particular to you! As you've read this book, what feels like one manageable change you could integrate into your life? What other sorts of challenges feel as though they will require the most courage and energy from you?

ADVENTURE CHALLENGE: Embrace one practice this week as a spiritual discipline that will free you to be for others.

THE FINAL CHALLENGE

Mark 2:13-15 says:

> Jesus went out again beside the sea; the whole crowd gathered around him, and he taught them. As he was walking along, he saw Levi son of Alphaeus sitting at the tax booth, and he said to him, "Follow me." And he got up and followed him. And as he sat at dinner in Levi's house, many tax collectors and sinners were also sitting with Jesus and his disciples—for there were many who followed him.

Imagine that you are sitting at your regular work when Jesus invites you, as he invited Levi, "Come with me." Close your eyes and imagine where—or to whom—Jesus is leading you right now. Can you discern a first step that Jesus is inviting you to take as you follow him toward the ones his Father loves?

ADVENTURE CHALLENGE: Commit to inviting one person you know just peripherally right now—a housekeeper, a barista, a janitor, a church member—to join you for dinner in your home. Then just wait and see what God might have up his divine sleeve.

Remember, just choose *one* of these adventure challenges to embrace this week!

NOTES

Chapter 2: Bible

page 35   "When I look critically at my life": Henri Nouwen, *The Road to Daybreak: A Spiritual Journal* (New York: Image, 1990), pp. 71-72.

pages 35-36 "Selling what you own": Ibid., p. 46.

Chapter 5: Stranger

page 53   "Every community has people": Christopher Heuertz and Christine Pohl, *Friendship at the Margins: Discovering Mutuality in Service and Mission,* Resources for Reconciliation (Downers Grove, Ill.: InterVarsity Press, 2010), p. 19.

page 55   "In meetings with her, she would frequently say": Ibid., p. 76.

Chapter 7: Introverts

page 62   "A subtle but insidious message": Adam McHugh, *Introverts in the Church: Finding Our Place in an Extroverted Culture* (Downers Grove, Ill.: InterVarsity Press, 2009), p. 13.

Chapter 8: Men

page 71   "We have some of the same James and John qualities": Martin Luther King Jr., "The Drum Major Instinct" (sermon, Ebenezer Baptist Church, Atlanta, Ga., February 4, 1968).

Chapter 9: Women

page 78   A feature in my city's: Emily Matchar, "Feminists Who Can," *Independent Weekly*, Wednesday, August 25, 2010.

Chapter 16: Urban

pages 125-26 "If we are inconvenienced or annoyed" and "Living in closer proximity": Eric Jacobsen, *Sidewalks in the Kingdom: New Urbanism and the Christian Faith* (Grand Rapids: Brazos, 2003), p. 28.

Chapter 22: Parent

page 165   "We're showing that you can redefine": Joseph Salwen, in Hannah and Kevin Salwen, *The Power of Half: One Family's Decision to Stop Taking and Start Giving Back* (New York: Mariner Books, 2010), p. 108.

Chapter 25: Spend Less

page 179   "One day a mother came to our apartment": Herta Janzen, in Doris Janzen Longacre, *Living More with Less,* ed. Valerie Weaver-Zercher, 30th anniversary ed. (Scottdale, Penn.: Herald Press, 2010), p. 141.

page 183   "North Americans find it very hard to believe": Bertha Beachy, in ibid., p. 38.

Chapter 29: Influence

page 208   "The place God calls you to": Frederick Buechner, *Wishful Thinking: A Seeker's ABC* (New York: HarperSanFrancisco, 1993), p. 119.

Chapter 30: Transformation

page 216   "Jesus' life is marked": Henri Nouwen, *The Road to Daybreak: A Spiritual Journal* (New York: Image, 1990), p. 149.

Hey reader,

I'm absolutely delighted that you're noodling on the ways that God is calling *you* to engage with a world in need right where you are.

If this book has sparked any new ideas in your noggin, conviction in your heart or action in your body, I—and our fellow adventurers!—want to know about it! Please email ShareOneSmallThing@gmail.com to report how you recognized an opportunity to move toward someone on the world's margins, or were blessed when another crossed barriers to move toward you!

If you found *Small Things* to be helpful, share it with a friend—or study it as a group!—so that you can support and encourage one another in this adventure of a lifetime.

Cheering you on,
Margot

P.S. Friend me at www.facebook.com/Margot and learn more at www.MargotStarbuck.com!